Also by Cassie Premo Steele

Poetry

Ruin

This is how honey runs

The Pomegranate Papers

Musical Poetry

This is how honey runs

The Pomegranate Songs

Nonfiction

Moon Days

We Heal from Memory

My Peace

Easyhard

Fiction

Shamrock and Lotus

Wednesday

for Laura –

with great gratitude

for your commitments to

poetry and feminism!

Cassie Premo Steele

and Facebook Friends

July 14, 2013

ISBN 978-1-936373-40-6
Published in the United States by Unbound Content, LLC, Englewood, NJ.
Cover art: ©2013, by Tamela Spires
Cover design: Susanne Kappler
Author photo: ©2013, by Susanne Kappler

Wednesday

For friends everywhere

Table of Contents

July

August

September

October

An Introduction by Daniel Dowe
Many Years of Wednesdays Led to This One

Back in the early 1990s, many twenty-somethings in their first apartments had refrigerators strewn with magnetic poetry. During impromptu parties or Saturday movie nights, some guest would invariably decide to take whatever words were not currently living as a line of dirty or sardonic or inspiring poetry and add his or her own message to the kitchen canvas. Sometimes, if the combination of words were clever enough, these little phrases or even poems would stay up for weeks or months, but usually, a new party and a drunken friend would mean new combinations and new phrases to ponder or giggle over—since they were often about sex.

What made these sets of magnets fun was their inherent collaborative nature. Sure, they could be totally silly or slightly provocative or even shocking—but they were an amalgam of the group that lived there or visited there on a regular basis. They were an aggregate of thoughts and wishes that any group of friends had at any given time. And everyone who grabbed a beer or soda got to read, react, and perhaps join in.

For most poets, writing poetry is a generally solitary pursuit. They might be pleased to share it later—at a slam, in a chapbook, at a coffeehouse reading—but the creation is usually done all alone. Most of us like it that way—we get in some great wavelength or creative mindset and try our hardest to describe whatever precise points of life's many mysteries we are trying to decipher and explain.

Cassie Premo Steele has certainly been one of those writers— working hard in her backyard near the brook, in her writer's studio with its flowers and many windows, or on a walk on a dewy

Columbia morning. She's written many books and many poems this way—like her fellow poets—crafting and building and creating. Luckily for us and for her, she's been able to share her work—and she's warm and wonderful at this. She's got a great voice for a poetry reading—like a good cabernet.

But if you've known Cassie for as long as I have, and it's now over twenty years, you also know that Cassie is a leader and a corraller and a gatherer of souls. Back when she was at the University of Virginia and then at the University of South Carolina and Emory University, Cassie amassed a large group of friends and cohorts, practicing community service and aiming for positive social change.

Therefore, it's natural (and I use this word deliberately, since she told me the very first poem in this book was in response to the BP disaster in the Gulf) that Cassie as a writer would eventually find a way to be collaborative about her poetry—and not just with one or two other writers—but with many. Since June 2010, Cassie has been inviting her friends, fellow artists, clients, and colleagues to join her in a poetry writing collaboration. Every Wednesday, she asks friends to add a word to a Facebook thread—and by the middle of that day, she takes whatever she gets—and the choices can really vary sometimes—and constructs a poem that somehow weaves the spirit and the intentions of all those words and all those who participated.

The results are what follow in this book. You'll see a whole range of subjects and ideas. Cassie's friends have given her many parts of life to contemplate. I've been a faithful reader of these poems for a while now. I've seen people post words that seem impossible for anyone to form into any kind of poem—strictly scientific words, nonsense words, profane words—and yet Cassie has managed to use them all and find their inherent resonance.

Watching what people post as word suggestions has been interesting. While at times, some of those who are posting words seem to be trying to challenge her with some highly non-poetic choices like "razzmatazz" or "quotidian," most of her collaborators have, over time, consulted the words that others have already posted and added their own, keeping up a kind of almost symphonic intention; they wanted to keep the same music going but maybe thought of something a woodwind or a brass or a bagpipe might say.

Once Cassie has posted the poem, her collaborators usually respond enthusiastically. Often they respond just with praise for the poem but just as often with their own thoughts and insights—so that the poem ends up almost spilling over onto a lengthy Facebook thread—a still expanding collaboration.

What many of Cassie's collaborators probably do not fully realize is just what a challenge it can be to write these poems. I've been a guest poet on a couple of occasions, so I know how hard it can be to write a poem that encompasses words from twenty or more different people. What I learned, however, is the importance of getting out of the way of the poem and the process, of letting these words, which may at first seem incongruous, find their way to new connections and new insights about life. It may seem cliché, but letting the creative process work with these collaborations is one of the most valuable lessons the Wordy Wednesday poems give. Even the most solitary poet still writes with all kinds of people present—as we speak to and consider all the people we have ever known and loved.

What Cassie Premo Steele has found is that we are social animals, as well as poets, and that we all love to participate and have a say. Usually the noisiness of life and the din of so many voices keep that from being practical. But every Wednesday, on Cassie's Facebook thread, a group of minds and hearts and spirits come together, and they make art and music, and yes, poetry together— all with some silent urging for wholeness working wonders, and yet with their own humorous, clever, social, political, enigmatic, and spiritual results.

In the Beginning

You, Witches and Dancers and Terminal Ones, This One's for You

You, deciduous witch.
I see you coming and
going like this, at esbat
gatherings on full moon
nights. It will be all right.

And you, man, enamored
of other men. You long
to savor the sticky succor
until sleepy. Go on,
sweetheart. Give in.

You, wavering between
truculent and blissful,
giving the one who
adored you a mouthful.
Be still. Be mindful.

You, carrying the word
terminal in a perpetual wallop
across your back. Stop that.
No need to wallow.
I absolve you.

Speaking of clemency,
I turn to you, silver dancer
who spins in ecstasy. To be
a siren is no sin. I give you
hugs and a kiss. Fly. Be sexy.

And then there's you,
abject one in anonymity,

anxious over this unseasonal
warm weather. Take off your
sweater. Sequined is better.

And you, you erudite boob
pawning obsessed exclusion
as your best offer. Allow for
emersion from your sea. Come up.
It is nourishment you are after.

All of you, the sensuous and
obsessed, the groovy and skittish,
you fascinate me far beyond curiosity.
I samba in gratitude, right here,
every Wednesday, in your honor.

Co-Created with Diane Charuhas Gould, Mary Hutchins Harris, Libby
Bussinah, Kendal Turner, Caroline Flow, Kathie Turner, Barbara H Thomson,
Veronica Dangerfield, Anastasia Shaw, Stacey Hamilton, Louise M Greer,
Pamila Lorentz, Russ Eidson, Al Black, Daves Here Man, Daniel Dowe, Kris
Friend, Mike Amason, Debbie Turner, James St John, Elizabeth JoAnn Sumner
Jones, Gail McGrail Glasser, Shannon Ivey Jones, Lisa Rynex Ragusa, Amy
Coquillard, Worthy Branson Evans, Helen Summer, Lisa Nielsen, Trish Vicino,
Cathi Christmus, Lisabeth Saunders Medlock, Barbie Smith Mathis, Lan Ngoc
Hoang, Jeanette Cheezum, Susanne Kappler, Marguerite O'Brien, Bruce Clark,
Alison Beard

January

Begin

Going from darkness to joy
is not like opening a toy
under the tree. Usually,

it's like taking the tree
to the curb and standing there
openhanded, undisturbed.

Faith is a commitment.
Beyond the Hallelujah!
to the soulfire within.

Begin.

Take a flashlight to the yard.
See the sentient beings working
hard and give them a Mwa!

Be overcome with awe.
Some are beheaded, some
are demure, some in a rage.

We can't all act our age.
The Earth is on a fiscal
cliff, too, you know.

4 1/2 billion years and
it's beginning to show.
She birthed humans

200,000 years ago
in a steampunk dance.
We have been in a trance

ever since, daring to think
she is not our mother but
a hobgoblin, and all it takes

to make a dawn is to turn
the lights on. Life on earth
is an accomplishment, folks.

Let's try this intention
on for size: Take your serpent
and turbulence and panic

and all those who denigrate
your daring to be calm
and throw it to a tree.

Remember what I said for you
to do to change into the faith
and joy within?

Begin.

Do it again. Take the opportunity.
This is the year of felicity.
Dance with me.

Co-Created with Marguerite O'Brien, Val Ryan, Caroline Flow, James J Lundy Jr, Alison Beard, Lisa Rynex Ragusa, Kris Friend, Barbie Smith Mathis, Bianca Premo, Louise M Greer, Duna Miller, Worthy Branson Evans, Mike Amason, Debbie Turner, Lisa Nielsen, Kezia Slaughter, Jeanette Gallagher, Tamela Spires Hastie, Tracy Gould Sheinin, Julianna Temple-Roberts, Helen Summer, Joyce Norman, Jeanne Porter Ashley, Sandy Mau, Alan Altshuld, Amaryllis Turman, Clarissa McFairy, Anastasia Shaw, Al Black, Lan Ngoc Hoang, Casey Catherine Moore, Amy Coquillard, Barbara H Thomson, Libby Bussinah, Lisabeth Saunders Medlock, Bruce Clark

Here We Are

It seems incredible. Here we are,
in the new year. I didn't believe the hype,
though the doomsayers were so
thorough. Talk of hoarding seeds
and solar flares left me with ennui
and seemed, frankly, a bit squirrelly.
I would rather trust in community
the way my mother says my
grandmother did in the 30s:
ignoring the mayhem, believing
in hope, giving up the expectation
of what will be on the plate and
making a ragu out of what together
the neighbors' gardens could make.
English is not a language of
agglutination, but many of us come
from one, and all of us are living
on land that once belonged to them.
It is winter now, and cold, and
already the newness of the year
has dissipated. Even though the
holidays are over, some of us are
still running, exhausted. Some
are in bed with a migraine,
some are watching depraved
indifference on the television and
turning into alabaster. Some are
longing to go even faster, and
some are buying into a syndicate.
None of this will last very long,
though. The end is coming yet.
My two predictions for this year
are wonderful and vague and

full of sense: 1. No solution
is the solution except the natural
constitution. And 2. What is eclectic
is the essence of what will take us,
mindfully, into the future tense
of who we are and what we do.
Us. Them. Together. Me. You.

Co-Created with Kris Friend, Daniel Dowe, Renee Bergeron, Amy Coquillard, Katherine Beth LaPrad, Doug Graul, Tina Taylor Newton, Betty Cobb Gurnell, Ellen Parker Dukes, Kezia Slaughter, Coralee Harris, Charlotte Koon Ehney, Ann Poling, Casey Catherine Moore, Gail McGrail Glasser, Linda Tina Maldonado, Al Black, Cara Holman, Elizabeth Akin Stelling, Oma Boyd, Marguerite O'Brien, Julianna Temple-Roberts, Lisa Nielsen, Louise M Greer

Thirteen Ways of Looking at Winter

I
Among twelve long months,
Retrograde happens
At least once.

II
I am slow,
Like a planet
That needs an incentive.

III
The beloved trees sway in the winter wind.
It is a dance of reverence.

IV
Snow and ice
Are one.
Snow and a fountain, with reluctance,
Are one.

V
I do not know which to prefer,
The emotion of this moment
Or the coming spring,
This blissful freeze
Or anticipation.

VI
Thoughts pepper my mind
With hopes of being
Better.

VII
O women in the bistro,
Do you not see the season
Swirling at your feet
And longing
For your attention?

VIII
I know what it means
To ruffle feathers
As a way of staying warm;
But I know, too,
That the feathers know
More than I know.

IX
When the winter flies out this year,
It will be no different
Than other kinds of leaving.

X
At the sight of buds
Blushing on the trees,
Even the wind
Would disdain this season.

XI
I once rode to Connecticut
And discovered mountains.
I'd been expecting flat land.
The vision was a way to mend
What had been broken.

XII
The light is moving behind milky skies.
The winter must be easing.

XIII
It was winter all season.
There was snow
And the promise of snow.
The cardinal sat
In the pear tree all day.

Co-Created with Tammy Wilkins Jenkins, Southcarolina Artists, Corey Mesler, Amsa Yoga, Robin Zavada, Lisa Nielsen, Jeanette Cheezum, MaryAnn Joseph, Kimberley Goeglein Puryear, Stacey Hamilton, Duna Miller, Coralee Harris, Elizabeth Akin Stelling, Cindi Boiter, Grace Pickens Burns, Bonnie Goldberg

Cassie Premo Steele

My Daughter Asks Me About Serendipity

My daughter asks me about serendipity
and I say it's when you have feelings

Of integrity (like, no need to boast, but
it's all cool) and they form a circle

With grace. That's pretty slippery, Mom,
she says. I think I'll check the dictionary.

And with the resolve of an 11-year-old girl,
she curls up with the book and is content

to let her dormant braincells come awake.
I think about baking a cake, remember

that I'm trying to get in shape, and
thank God again that we don't homeschool.

The science test on saponification is
Friday, and as much as I love soap,

I don't think I could draw the chemical
compound of it, let alone teach it.

My mind wanders back to serendipity,
and I think about the word "resolute."

How a writing client told me yesterday
it was going to be her word of the week,

and then it shows up first when I peek
at the Wordy Wednesday list, and I guess

34

this is how things work. There is magic
in words and chemicals and cake,

but you have to give them time to bake,
make the connection, add your mind,

allow that it is possible in the first place.
You have to be willing to look it up yourself.

Co Created with Coralee Harris, Robin Zavada, Tammy Wilkins Jenkins,
Rebecca C Jacobson, Kezia Slaughter, Jeralyn Vitale Wunderley, Katrina
Murphy, Christine Sahli Helms, Gail McGrail Glasser, Charlotte Koon, Amy
Coquillard, Annie Hitselberger Fell, Connie Benesh

Cassie Premo Steele

Things We Learned From This Morning's News

The economy is either salubrious or moving toward collapse.
It depends on whether your heart is in the present or the past.

Buchanan was both a candidate and a rescued captive.
It depends on when and where in this universe you live.

Pirates can be enemies or musicals or toys.
All are kinds of playthings and camouflage for boys.

Gabby can be happy and talkative or sweet and silent.
All are ways of healing with friendship after great violence.

Irene could have been an Irish immigration song or a hurricane.
Both are long pink tunnels after which home will never be the same.

Education standards are either rigorous or tepid.
It depends on whether you meander or let justice rule your head.

Primary choices render Florida voters fascinating or dysphoric.
It depends on whether you find fatty biscuits delicious or caloric.

Traffic on I-20 near Clemson Road is either scrunchy or endurable.
All the news is a combination of our synergy and what we find
believable.

Co-Created with Annie Marshall, Amy Alley, Daniel Dowe, Leisa Marie
Mounts, Candi Padgett, Mary Anne Farmer Tillman, Kris Friend, Zoe Viveca
Sumner, Kathryn Van Aernum, Lisa Gornicki Bolender, Christine Tapson,
Mary Ann Joseph, Kezia Slaughter, Katherine Beth LaPrad, Suzanne Kamata,
Kendal Turner, Kathryn Ramsby, Gail McGrail Glasser, Tamela Spires Hastie,
Tommy Lightfoot, Jeannie Pickett Eidson, Marguerite O'Brien, Trish Vicino,
Joyce Norman

The Waist Land

I. THE BURIAL OF THE BREAD

January is the cruelest month, marrying
the steamboat of our hunger with our desire
to be the phoenix that, this year, rises
from our flesh and flies.

On day one, we are the ninja who pilots
the airship. We eschew the Oreo
and communicate with central command:
yes, the blueberry is a miracle food!

We write down each morsel of mastication.
We think of the SHOW and finger our prostate,
we used to lie prostrate before coffee cake,
but no mo!

By week's end, we are kind and twirling.
In the mirror, we are loving. Life is a kind
of fête, our bellies will be smooth as mahogany,
we vow to have spunk and no regret.

II. A GAME OF CHASE

The masterpiece gets lonely in week three.
We stop for gas at Chevron and fantasize
about the tiny white donuts in packs inside,
so cheap, almost free. It's months to go
before our birthday, and while we would
more than anything like to look amazing!
by then (we imagine the comments on our
Facebook page under our photo and grin),
the truth is the mélange of protein powder

and fiber is wearing kind of thin. Thin—
HURRY UP PLEASE IT'S TIME
the driver behind us says with a beep.
Thin, we say to ourselves, as this desire's
nullification pulls us back from the deep
to our cars (the donuts were evil! we are saints!)
and we pull our cellphones from our
purses and press the buttons, hoping
our sisters will be there to commiserate.

III. THE ANATOMY SERMON

Here comes Valentine's Day. All that chocolate!
Put it away. Every spine has a foramen (plural,
foramina): the place where nerves and such go
through. We have a spine, too. We do.

We do not have a tail, and so we get a teacher
(she is so thin, so thin, there is no way we can
reach her, but we try, we try)

and she suggests we Google anatomy to learn
about ourselves in a more inside look and see.

Click click click
Flash flash flash flash
So rudely forced
Mort

Dead City
The puce disappointment of the ribs
Mr. John Doe, on a table
His wife and girlfriend still believe

they were the only one,
and here on the internet
his heart is splayed open and undone.

Is this all there is?
Is there nothing of the body we can trust?
Is there no preternatural reason for our being outside this flesh?
Are we not something more than meat, more than skin and pulp
beneath?

IV. DEATH BY CHOCOLATE

March comes. Earth warms. We wake
like daffodils inside the soil of our beds
and a thought disentangles inside our heads.
                              Size is superfluous
to those who see with wisdom's eyes.
We venerate Whitman, not for the size
(oh, desexualize!) of his thighs.
                              The vulture flies
and casts a shadow dark and sweet.
We get up and cut a wedge of cake and eat.

V. WHAT THE SUN SAID

After the blooms have come and gone
and summer's heat makes something cold
upon the tongue not only necessary but
healthful for the old and young, you sit
on the lounge chair by the pool, and with
it tipped back like this, your bikini
(yes, you did it, and it's pink, and
even your thirteen-year-old daughter

thinks it's cool)

And no fat
If there were fat
And no water
Or water
And no pool
This pink you
That here will coalesce
Would be fantasy
And fool

Who is the third who walks always beside you?
Girlfriend, we talk and laugh and carry on
but behind your eyes I hear the song
of another siren
who sings,
Not fine. Not fine.
Eat less.
Outshine.

And I watch you waste away with apathy.
Please.
HURRY UP PLEASE IT'S TIME

You are tremendous.
Do you know what that means?

MA
Take: What have you been given?
My friend, put it to your lips.

MA
Eat: While we ignore the poverty
of those around us, is it not a sin to stop?

MA
Live: This is what the sun says
(and the son, and the sloe fizz.)

How come every time you come around
My London London Bridge want to go down

Là, tout n'est qu'ordre et beauté,
Luxe, calme et volupté. Oh, swallow, swallow
My friend, my brother, sister, and myself.
These fragments of yourself are no help.
You are not a thing upon a shelf.
You are alive. You have a home.
Take. Eat. Live.

Om   Om   Om

Co-Created with Kate Fox, Annmarie Lockhart, Rachel Onley, Rachal Hatton, Robert Lewis, Amaryllis Turman, Casey Catherine Moore, KC Bosch, Louise M Greer, Cheryl Anne Cudmore, Kezia Slaughter, Joyce Norman, James St John, Kristi Krumnow Fuhriman, Daves Here Man, Amy Coquillard, Tamela Spires Hastie, Caroline Flow, Vale N Adan, Leisa Marie Mounts, Camille Richardson, Mary Hutchins Harris, Duna Miller, Sandy Mau, Al Black, Lisa Nielsen, Debbie Turner, Julianna Temple-Roberts, Lan Ngoc Hoang, Anastasia Shaw, Susanne Kappler, Gail McGrail Glasser, Linda Tina Maldonado, Barbara H Thomson, Helen Summer, Marguerite O'Brien, Bruce Clark, Lisabeth Saunders Medlock, Trish Vicino, Cindy Patterson, Barbie Smith Mathis, Southcarolina Artists, Libby Bussinah, Kris Friend, Steve Hait

Align

Somewhere there is snowflake silence.
Somewhere else there is a womb caress.

I began this poem before dawn.
Then I went to get dressed.

On one side of the world, it is sweltering.
In 556 places, people encourage the mess.

I went for a walk at dewy sunrise.
At this uplift time, the birdsong is best.

Somewhere someone is eating a clementine.
Somewhere else bravery is climbing up a spine.

Above me, a plane made a bright white line.
Then another came counter and created an X.

On one side of the world, the sun enters creation.
In 566 places, human event and meaning align.

The X formed whiskers or a polarized sign.
An inward message to simplify and be fine.

Somewhere there is a hidden desire.
Somewhere else people hesitate.

Suddenly anthropomorphic sky was suffused
with light. And I really began to run.

On one side of the world, love is eternal.
In 557 places, a girl wearing a tutu is impatient.

Today is my mother-in-law's birthday.
When she died, my husband became a heart patient.

Somewhere there is a war going on.
Somewhere else people step out of a noose.

My lungs burned as I put my hand on the knob.
My husband was calmly eating pamplemousse.

On one side of the world, there is endless hope.
In 558 places, people try to cope without a job.

I took this picture with my heart beating.
I wanted to show it to you and make your heart throb.

Somewhere there is peace and harmony and calm.
Somewhere else people reconcile and take apart bombs.

Co-Created with Cara Holman, Amaryllis Turman, Julianna Temple-Roberts, Annie Marshall, Christine Tapson, Daniel Dowe, Amy Coquillard, Tommy Lightfoot, Kris Friend, Jessica Leigh Wells, Katherine Beth LaPrad, Mildred Speidel, Elizabeth Akin Stelling, Kezia Slaughter, Casey Catherine Moore, Jeannie Pickett Eidson, Gail McGrail Glasser, Kathryn Van Aernum, Tammy Wilkins Jenkins, Lisa Nielsen, Prajna Nash, Annmarie Lockhart, Louise M Greer, Leisa Marie Mounts, Janeen Musselman, Nicole Thompson-Smith, Karla Turner, Marguerite O'Brien, Beverley Burchell Hardman

Do This

You ask me how to make your dreams come true.
Don't be a dunce. Of course I know what to do.
But don't get excited. I don't have commandments,
a handy list to calculate the common denominator
of fear over glue. You know me by now. I'm a guru.
So I'll say: Get in the saddle. Be a ninja. Listen to
a waterfall. Play. And you'll look at me as if I'm
speaking Swahili instead of bonhomie and say, "Hey!
Are you on morphine? Give me some concrete
perspective here! This is my dream!" And I become
redundant (at least to me) and start to spell it out.
Even the classifieds are not in a paper anymore.
Stop the shameless selling. Inspiration is not a
formula to tout. Bazinga is funny because Sheldon
does not shout. Grateful is the gateway to be wise.
You don't need an optometrist to see with new eyes.
Do what mothers do: be quiet for a long time for
development to materialize. Find a tribe. If the one
you are in is a jailer, exonerate yourself. Let the
revolution catalyze. Come out. The opposite is
homicide. It's about a worldview. Ideas start inside.
Go into the dumpling of your skin and find
integrity within. It doesn't take a psychic (or if it
does, she only helps because she's punctilious).
You don't need what you think you must have: not
that job, that man, that title, that money, that
layaway plan. You can't implant metamorphosis.
Even Athena wore an aegis. It was to protect her
from this: toxicity, duplicity, and complicity.
All the things that split. Dreams are born in unity.

Wednesday

Wear your shield as Athena did, and you, too,
can grow her dream of this: democracy, domesticity,
felicity, simplicity, authenticity and synchronicity.
Now stop putzing. Do this. Do. Right now. You.

Co-Created with Pamila Lorentz, Alison Beard, Janeen Musselman, Mary Ann Joseph, Joyce Norman, Anastasia Shaw, Stephen Owen, Barbie Smith Mathis, Lisa Gornicki Bolender, Marguerite O'Brien, Kathie Turner, Amaryllis Turman, Caroline Flow, Kris Friend, Jeanette Cheezum, Mike Amason, Worthy Branson Evans, Louise M Greer, Jennifer Smith Dearing, Lisa Nielsen, Daves Here Man, Bonnie Goldberg, Rachel Onley, Jeanne Porter, Ashley Kristi Krumnow Fuhriman, Ann Poling, Tammy Wilkins Jenkins, Al Black, Duna Miller, Tommy Lightfoot, Camille Richardson, Lan Ngoc Hoang, Sandy Mau, Barbara H Thomson, Cheryl Anne Cudmore, Elizabeth JoAnn Sumner Jones, Tamela Spires Hastie, Gail McGrail Glasser, Julianna Temple-Roberts, Leisa Marie Mounts

February

Love From One to Eight and Eighty

Year one: You learn the hopelessness of latching on.
Year ten: You anticipate when your mother will be gone.

Year two: You dream of the circus, the roustabouts adopting you.
Year twenty: You dream of the feisty guy in chemistry seeing you anew.

Year three: You are beginning to think your mother is a spy.
Year thirty: This is beginning to be exhausting and you don't know why.

Year four: You can write the word LOVE on a Valentine.
Year forty: You realize you can replenish and not give all the time.

Year five: You entrain your parents to give in before you scream.
Year fifty: You can compensate for anything with ice cream.

Year six: Legos, ponies, pink and paint: what you love you glorify.
Year sixty: You meet women who tell you Shekinah is passing by.

Year seven: Someone dies. Life is short. You are sad.
Year seventy: Someone dies. Life is wondrous. You are sad, yet glad.

Year eight: You give your Colorforms to your sister.
Year eighty: You put jonquils on your mister. Sad, yet glad again.

Co-Created with Robin Zavada, Kathleen Capehart, Coralee Harris, Gail McGrail Glasser, Lizzie Thomas, Alissa McElreath, Karen Fuchs, Corey Mesler, Kimberley Goeglein Puryear, Stacey Hamilton, Tamela Spires Hastie, Zoe Pruitt Owen, Kezia Slaughter, Charlotte Koon Ehney, Lisa Nielsen, Duna Miller

Love Song at Middle Age

I thought I'd have a groupie or two by now.
I only have a grouper on my plate. How

did the time dissipate? I used to lollygag
and now when I drag a cigarette, I gag.

I want a tryst with you. It's true.
My ethmoid bone separates my brain from goo,

but sinus medication will not do. Tangled
is my mind when you are kind. I am jangled,

bewitched, bothered and bewildered.
When you walked away, you said Namaste

and I only wanted you to stay. I burned
for you and you left me in a cinder. Will I learn

that jellyfish cannot survive the dish
of a sweltering pond for long? I wish

to be entwined with you. No, sir, too much wine
has not been served. William Blake is fine,

but we are not in school. Give me spicy truth.
Give me the geometry of lines we can't undo.

Give me a meaning and a bramble. Let us bleed.
Hold on to me, your silken tightwire. Do not heed

the height. Let your body feel transfiguration.
Not at the knees. Get up and come with me in liberation.

Co-Created with Michele E. Hutchinson, Annmarie Lockhart, Carol Agnew Black, Kelly Rametta, Carla Blankenship Mangine, Kendal Turner, Feili Tu-Keefner, Veronica Dangerfield, Cara Holman, Julianna Temple-Roberts, Russ Eidson, Kris Friend, Kate Fox, Joyce Norman

Some Love

Some love just helps us to grow, gets us another
birthday, each year is a lake and we are the boat.
And some love bursts like a supernova,
illuminates everything in its torrential glow.
But some love is a cockroach, we crawl down
below on our bellies while we scurry to cope.
Some love is a blue bowl, less about connection
than what happens within. And some love is
all about patience and time, reconciliation, a cello
and bow. Some love is plumeria, scattered in a pond,
left there to float. Some love is indifferent, given
so freely it falls in fatigue. And some love we justify,
taking scissors, we learn how to prune. Some love
starts in *espoir*, and hope turns to dupe all too soon.
Some love is benevolent, an affirmation of hips.
Some love is frogsong and whippoorwill, a symphony
of rain and lunar eclipse. And some love is appetence,
a thunderous shower of hunger we bring to our lips.

Co-Created with Kezia Slaughter, Lisa Gornicki Bolender, Ellen Parker Dukes,
Russ Eidson, Lizzie Thomas, Feili Tu, Joyce Norman, Leisa Marie Mounts,
Coralee Harris, Vicky Saye Henderson, Daniel Dowe, Lisa Nielsen, Louise
M Greer, Cara Holman, Michael Tweed, Annmarie Lockhart, Mary Ann
Joseph, Duna Miller, Grace Pickens Burns, Jeannie Pickett Eidson, Al Black,
Katherine Beth LaPrad, Stacey Hamilton, Kathy Paget, Kris Friend, Debbie
Turner, Christine Tapson, Kate Fox, Sandrine Dupon, Betty Cobb Gurnell,
Libby Bussinah

What Is Calling for Blessing in You?

happenstance happens   when we least expect it.
                                we must remain calm.
        what is calling for blessing in you?
a blizzard of ice   when we tire of being dormant.
  retreat   when we long for forgiveness.
all growth comes from somewhere deep.
                         everything is mutable.
the groundhog   is not the only one with dreams of sleep.
  every answer leads to the limbo of more questions.
the earth   gets poked into effusiveness every year.
        what is calling for blessing in you?
put down   your tea and walk into the burgeoning world.
  we get rebirth when we give an ounce.
bullets   are frangible when they shatter.
             souls bounce.

what is calling for blessing in you?

Co-Created with Charlotte Koon Ehney, Ray Brown, Amy Coquillard, Janeen Musselman, Zoe Pruitt Owen, Daniel Dowe, Annmarie Lockhart, Lisa Nielsen, Libby Bernardin, Duna Miller, Kimberley Goeglein Puryear, Betty Cobb Gurnell, Corey Mesler, Stacey Hamilton

How She Dances

she dances fabulous, like the dawn.
her body is the cause of loverly
possibilities. it is her platform.
she uses laconicism to say much.
her awakening comes with the moon.
she is a subliminal minx in the room.
occasionally she goes on a bender
and gets audacious. it depends on
the circumstance. she is a dancer,
and you can't stop her, but later
she is humble, lies low like a fish,
beyond sleepy, just exhausted
in her pond. and then she rises,
lithe like a flamingo (which i
saw fly once in france and
it was mysterious and pink and
so curious it made me want
to dance the tango until dawn).
the karma of a dancer is that
of the velveteen rabbit, we are
lunar and snowy and have a
pathological need to be real
and belong. come on, we say
to the world. let's dance!
get up! join in! come on!

Co-Created with Corrie Struble, Virginia Clare Andrews, Amaryllis Turman, Joyce Norman, Gail McGrail Glasser, Coralee Harris, Brett Sheftman, Tracy Gould Sheinin, Mary Ann Joseph, Tina Taylor Newton, Kate Fox, Elizabeth Akin Stelling, Katherine Beth LaPrad, Leisa Marie Mounts, Grace Pickens Burns, Cara Holman, Lisa Nielsen, Carol Agnew Black, Casey Catherine Moore, Ellen Parker Dukes, Veronica Dangerfield, Louise M Greer, Jeanette Gallagher, Janeen Musselman, Kezia Slaughter, Audrey Horton Shifflett, Betty Cobb Gurnell, Nicole Thompson-Smith

After Love

All I wanted to eat
yesterday was bacon

It was salt and protein
masquerading as fat

Sometimes my heart wants some
chocolate, I get that.

I look best in fuchsia
lingerie, I feel best

when slurping wine and cheese.
Epic thirst engenders

dull thinking. Trust hunger.
He is noble and sincere.

Keep eating until all
is mended. Your body

is not a lost phantom.
She is just fine right here.

Co-Created with Lisa Gornicki Bolender, Foster Hunter, Kendal Turner, Annmarie Lockhart, Lisa Nielsen, Joyce Norman, Jessica Leigh Wells, Cara Holman, Louise M Greer, Linda Tina Maldonado, Kathryn Van Aernum, Elizabeth Akin Stelling, Kezia Slaughter, Jeannie Pickett Eidson, Duna Miller, Gail McGrail Glasser, Ellen Parker Dukes, Norma Jeane Tiner, Kris Friend

My Stroke of Luck

What a way to transpose Lenten belief.
Instead of chocolate, it's my brain I gave up.
Good grief.

Humble your spirit before God,
said the priest. I was fraught.
I did nod.

I was alone in the hospital.
It was night. He had oil.
I gave gratitude.

Then rose the opportunity for attitude.
To hell with meditation, I said,
and started breathing.

This is growth, said a friend.
This is truth, said another.
Renew, said my mom.

I just wanted my own bed.
And a good meal.
And my daughter.

In all honesty? I did leap.
I am Irish. We like to reach
across oceans.

But I refuse to believe in myself as a cause,
or an action, or a rhetorical
lack of fidelity.

Wednesday

I am content to pray for less pressure
in the plinth my head
sits upon centrally.

I am willing to give up garrulous
in order to keep going on this
perilous journey.

I know now what the deep Ahhh
is worth. I will keep digging. I am
the diamond I will unearth.

Co-Created with Gail McGrail Glasser, Russ Eidson, Lisa Nielsen, Kimberley
Goeglein Puryear, Debbie Turner, Christine Tapson, Kris Friend, Coralee Harris,
Betty Cobb Gurnell, Kathryn Ramsby, Rebecca C Jacobson, Kezia Slaughter,
Tamela Spires Hastie, Ann Poling, Leisa Marie Mounts, Diane Hare, Elaine
Cooper, Trish Vicino, Mary Ann Joseph, Tammy Wilkins Jenkins, Steven
Cardinal, Marguerite O'Brien, Karla Turner, Ellen Parker Dukes

The True Seminary

The correlation between sunshine and my faith is spurious.
The increase in my courage after motherhood was curious.

That an inhibitor is necessary for healing makes me furious.
That death is a way to metamorphose is beyond mysterious.

Grace is a corroded anchor in an incandescent sea.
Souls are both coal and crystal longing for ecstasy.

My Manhattan mind might envision heaven as a luxurious
hotel with an open kitchen; a wiser dreamer knows that this is fiction.

Silence is the true seminary. The room of glory may be as big as
Texas, but it is empty. Love is less resplendent than cozy.

If we want to know the face of God in this gloaming world,
we must remind ourselves that countenance is both a noun and verb.

Let us not pray to fulfill the needs of some great list, but to be gentle.
Let us hope that God is still smitten with us as He was when we were little.

Co-Created with Julie E. Bloemeke, Betty Cobb Gurnell, Daniel Dowe, Amsa Yoga, Corey Mesler, Virginia Clare Andrews, Caroline Hatchell, Grace Pickens Burns, Tammy Wilkins Jenkins, Kezia Slaughter, Wilma Margono, Kathryn Ramsby, Lisa Nielsen, Mary Ann Joseph, Kimberley Goeglein Puryear, Duna Miller, Kate Fox, Annie Hitselberger Fell, Nicole and Rhonda Thompson-Smith, Janeen Musselman, Ellen Kline McLeod, Melissa Buckner, Brooke Pippen Compton, Cindi Boiter

March

March Morning

Winter's time of fasting
is almost at an end.
Sunshine's voice is singing,
"Transcend. Transcend."

At dawn my daughter shows me
petals in her hand
like counterfeit diamonds
stolen from the land.

The cold and gray retreat
in early bright spring air.
The apple branches
are festooned with flower hair.

I see the sky above is rosy pink
with sailors and their warnings.
She is confounded by this story
and the prophecy of mornings.

With intrigue, she asks me,
"What will the sky be tonight?"
And I tell her that the answer
can only be revealed on sight.

I wonder how much longer
she will think I hold solutions.
I am winter. She is spring.
Every season has its evolution.

Robust robins pick the
grass with gratitude.
Even the saffron lion
gives up his attitude.

Co-Created with Wilma Margono, Kezia Slaughter, Lisa Nielsen, Kimberley
Goeglein Puryear, Annie Hitselberger Fell, Elizabeth Akin Stelling, Al Black,
Duna Miller, Coralee Harris, Mildred Speidel, Sunita Dhurandhar, Grace
Pickens Burns, Southcarolina Artists

The Motion of Rain

The motion of rain is more than fluid.
It deconstructs the air as it tries to
beckon us to something deeper,
a tempered heart to persevere
through all that has splintered and
come apart. This is reconciliation:
taking our bodies, like wet and
wounded dogs, away from the
street and into a place of peace.
The pictures the soldiers took
were a way of making lucid,
maybe, what they'd done so
later someone would know
exactly how much was needed
to forgive. Only something limpid
can be seen through; everything
else is an excuse to overlook.
The grey Paris skies and rain
above London and Washington
join our longing here, wherever we are,
in a prayer for breaking through.

Co-Created with Wilma Margono, Daniel Dowe, Kimberley Goeglein Puryear,
Kim Lovelace McMahon, Christi Stewart, Virginia Clare Andrews, Kezia
Slaughter, Annmarie Lockhart, Gail McGrail Glasser, Christopher Allen,
Charlotte Koon Ehney, Mary Ann Joseph, Copeland Kapp, Annie Hitselberger
Fell, Carol Agnew Black

Water Is

Water is an indigo lover with
the capacity for diplomacy as she
opens her gorge in anticipation
of the sweet juice of her fruit.

Water, combined with a seat
too long in the saddle, is
also the ingredient for fungus.
Cut your beard. Let in the light.

Water can sharpen your knife
and achieve evisceration like a
facist. She has this ability because
she works with unconditional purity.

Water can even clean blight.
She is not compassionate in the
face of malcontent, wipes the
obstreperous away with her tide.

Water can be violent, a sniper
refusing hiatus, with her conjoined
twin, pride, a blossom in his hair,
stretched out and along for the ride.

Water brings atonement. Bliss of
this: soft acceptance brings fast
transformation. Believe even when
you're weary. Be like the ocean.

Water brings atonement, twice, thrice,
writing names in reverse in the Book
of Life, as many times as it takes to work.
Forgiving like the moon and the word.

Co-Created with Linda Tina Maldonado, Joyce Norman, Lisa Nielsen,
Nicole Thompson-Smith, Feili Tu-Keefner, Tammy Wilkins Jenkins, Janeen
Musselman, Casey Catherine Moore, James St John, Meg Haworth, Sandy
Mau, Tommy Lightfoot, Mildred Speidel, Rachel Lucas Muckenfuss, Al
Black, Veronica Dangerfield, Daniel Dowe, Kris Friend, Mike Amason,
Clint Wills, Trish Vicino, Tamela Spires Hastie, Barbie Smith Mathis,
Barbara H Thomson, Cindy Patterson, Nelly Travez Sommerkamp, Lisa
Rynex Ragusa, Liz Cunningham Delp, Cathy Carter-Scott, Marguerite
O'Brien, Kathie Turner, Jeanette Cheezum, Kathy Paget, Louise M Greer,
Steve Hait

This Violet Light

I want to be absolutely sleepless.
I want this violet light of moon night
to soak through my skin like an inculcation.

I want to blossom
in breathtaking faith.
But these are just wishes,

transient moments
like puddles compared to the estuary
of discombobulating morning news in the world.

My eggs get cold
as I hear the latest counts:
pollen, and bodies, and a diamond,

and then a message
about the wonders of Vicks,
and I wonder if there is a medicine for this.

Maybe something called Bueno!
with two possible side effects: chagrin
and hope. Take Bueno! to turn back the missiles,

dismantle the reactors,
mystify the energy misers and
allow all of us humans to begin over again.

Warm spring is the opposite
of pomegranate season, the fecund earth
is in no mood for relaxation, whatever gets planted

now has a chance
at forever, and so I take
something to keep me awake,

and I keep watching and waiting
for someone to admit their mistake.
I want to blossom in breathtaking faith.

Co-Created with Al Black, Jeanee Bourque, Corey Mesler, Rebecca Jacobson, Robin Zavada, Trish Vicino, Annmarie Lockhart, Lisa Nielsen, Coralee Harris, Amy Coquillard, Ashton Padgett, Tammy Wilkins Jenkins, Charlotte Koon Ehney, Gail McGrail, Grace Pickens Burns, Jeanette Cheezum, Janeen Musselman, Wilma Margono, Annie Hitselberger Fell, Elizabeth Akin Stelling, Roy Vasey, Caroline Grant, Southcarolina Artists, Mary Ogden Fersner, Janet Hull, Doris Snelgrove, Lydia Cortes, Jo Anne Simson

The Tao of the Earth

The world is a sacred vessel.

The Tao of the Earth is unfinished.
While we want scenes of serene hope,
dreams of possibilities and resilience,
the truth is random and cataclysmic
and heartbreak pops like popcorn
more often than we want to admit.

It should not be meddled with.

The Tao of the Earth is unfinished.
Katrina, Haiti, BP before this, and now
the world's womb smacking into Tokyo
while we listen in stereo, vaguely vowing
to help as we arrange our mélange
of belongings into our cars before work.

It should not be owned.

The Tao of the Earth is unfinished.
At the last minute, noticing raindrops,
we grab an umbrella, tie a child's shoe.
What would you have us do? we ask,
trembling at the overwhelming body
counts, and turning the volume down.

If you try to meddle with it, you will ruin it.

The Tao of the Earth is unfinished.
Should we jump suddenly
from the height of our lives

into the erratic movement of the ground?
Is this what the Earth is asking of us?
Where is the solution to be found?

If you try to own it, you will lose it.

(Lines in italics are from the 29th chapter of the *Tao Te Ching* by Lao Tzu.)

Co-Created with Robin Zavada, Betty Cobb Gurnell, Coralee Harris, Annmarie Lockhart, Kimberley Goeglein Puryear, Al Black, Kate Fox, Kezia Slaughter, Gail McGrail Glasser, Tammy Wilkins Jenkins, Janeen Musselman, Pamela Cauthen Meriwether, Annie Hitselberger Fell, Virginia Clare Andrew, Duna Miller, Carol Agnew Black, Elizabeth Akin Stelling, Lisa Nielsen

The Beatitudes of the Bestiary

1. Blessed is the poor ineffable stillness of the frog:
    for he shall forgive the persnickety absolutely.
    (For forgiveness means the kingdom of heaven is at hand.)

2. Blessed are the meek that present with the whisper of wings:
    for they shall possess precocious possibilities.
    (For such is the condition of possibility of the land.)

3. Blessed is the sultry rascal raven who mourns:
    for he shall receive a morning snuggle daily.
    (For a roar, not matter how cogent, is little comfort.)

4. Blessed is the cat that forgets her sister's symmetry:
    for she shall eat at the harvest before the frost.
    (For there are seasons to fill and seasons to sort.)

5. Blessed is the grasshopper who wants a life of immortality:
    for he shall deconstruct the stuck and wicked with mercy.
    (For thus aluminum sulfate transforms gutter to creek.)

6. Blessed is the dog after a fabulous bath:
    for he shall see the last remaining tick to lick.
    (For clean is not only a matter of eating what is sweet.)

7. Blessed is the lizard who skitters:
    for before him shall open the door of relief.
    (For letting go is the meaning of peace.)

8. Blessed is the monkey with the blatant character of a thief:
    for he shall reveal to us where we are weak.
    (For strength is holding on to what you seek.)

Co-Created with Lisa Gornicki Bolender, Pamela Cauthen Meriwether, Robin Zavada, Annmarie Lockhart, Steve Hait, Al Black, Marguerite O'Brien, Mary Ann Joseph, Leisa Marie Mounts, Laura Gaffke, Louise M Greer, Cathi Christmus, Debbie Turner, Kezia Slaughter, Lisa Nielsen, Elizabeth Akin Stelling, Anne Nichols Miller, Casey, Catherine Moore, Stephen Owen, Cheryl Thomas, Kathy Paget, Ellen Kline McLeod, Ellen Parker Dukes, Libby Bussinah, Janeen Musselman, Gail McGrail Glasser, Tina Taylor Newton, Brenda Ingbretsen Way, Liz Cunningham Delp, Mary Hutchins Harris, Kendal Turner, Trish Vicino, Katherine Beth LaPrad, Christy Everton, Annie Hitselberger Fell, Jeannie Pickett Eidson, Veronica Dangerfield

Syncopating

Before we are born, we open in peace and love,
moving from an amorphous state above

to a world that seems, at first, precarious.
Our parents are delirious. And dutiful.

We vie for their attention by being beautiful.
They look away when we become impetuous.

We eat Sugarbabies and play in pluff mud.
Eventually we wake to a dawn that is dangerous.

Each generation has their Pearl Harbor Day.
We fear another bomb is on its way.

We no longer see the blessing or the sparkle
in an elegant white pearl or celestial blue bay.

We spend our time on tollways, driving toward
employment or escrow. We swap spirit for

snappy at trade shows and refuse to grow.
And then our nerves start demyelinating.

The process is humiliating. And painful
and slow. It is a long lesson in waiting.

One day we remember our glow.
That pearl we were. The flow.

It is then we begin syncopating.
Living in Now, not a Long Time Ago.

Wednesday

Co-Created with Ellen Parker Dukes, Rebecca C Jacobson, Duna Miller, Annmarie Lockhart, Leisa Marie Mounts, Julianna Temple-Roberts, Christine Tapson, Amy Alley, Nicole Thompson-Smith, Janeen Musselman, Kimberley Goeglein Puryear, Amy Coquillard, Jessica Leigh Wells, Kathryn Ramsby, Grace Pickens Burns, Sara Eaton, Kezia Slaughter, Charlotte Koon Ehney, Lisa Nielsen, Tamela Spires Hastie, Kris Friend, Southcarolina Artists, Marguerite O'Brien

How You Survive

You think about triumph.
You drink your fearless
liquid and you feel the
insight curl up in your
belly like a gypsy
setting up camp:
You are resilient.
What you can survive
is limitless. You can
stand at the shoreline
of betrayal, watching
the thoughtless and
pessimistic do their
burning oil rig dance,
and you can sing,
brilliant. It is a song
of courage, hope, and
intuition, so powerful
it will instill the taste
of mineral on the tongue
of everyone who listens.
You are resilient, I say
again. You are a mountain
that cradles lacunae within.
When the oil rig people
approach you for ore,
instinct takes over, you
shout BOOM in their face,
your persistent spirit
rallies and you yell,
"You want some more?!?

Cuz I got a lot where that
came from!" and you place
a gardenia in your hair as they
disappear through your trap door.

Co-Created with Kate Fox, Kris Friend, Kezia Slaughter, Ellen Parker
Dukes, Louise M Greer, Charlotte Koon Ehney, Leisa Marie Mounts,
Gianluca D'Elia, Lisa Gornicki Bolender, Katherine Beth LaPrad, Diane
Hare, Sarah Endo, Tina Hirsig, Rebecca C Jacobson, Lisa Nielsen, Trish
Vicino, Marguerite O'Brien, Casey Catherine Moore, Grace Pickens
Burns, Pamela Cauthen Meriwether, Lizbeth Finn-Arnold, Annmarie
Lockhart, Laura Gaffke, Janeen Musselman, Gail McGrail Glasser, Alissa
McElreath

Dear Pope Francis

Hello and congratulations! You cut a fine shape
in that gown and you really know how to work
a crowd. There are a few things I want you to know,
though, Papa Francesco. And since knowledge
means taking us to the ledge, let me come out
with it so you can see: while I was relieved
to hear the name you'd taken, I also want to
take it beyond serendipity into revolution.

The Church took her time and taught me to
breathe. I grew up green on Sundays, saw
my mother try to be a good wife, and when
she crossed that bridge into annulment,
it was with your predecessor's sacrament.
Immaculata nuns taught me to love life.
We are part of all creation and the opposite
is hate—is what I heard Jesus saying as I
knelt and felt the words and music resonate.

But now there's an elephant in the room.
And it'll take a crane to lift it up and out.
What I'd like you to do is follow your model:
listen to the birds and hear what is vital.
Not the glory and greed and shenanigans—
not the subatomic gumption to exculpate
some and leave others in asphalt frustration.
No more hijinks of conquer and stratification.

It's time for action. My mother's word
for this (and she's a Eucharistic minister)
is sacrifice. What we mean by this is that
it's time for you to put your umbrella up

and include all of us in your shelter from
the slurp and rain. The gays. The women.
The ones you consider fallen. The ones
you cause such pain. What you need to
know is that we know how to disentangle
longing into some place very comfortable.
Beyond consolation into warmth without
the fuss. Transforming restless motion
into exuberant being: that's our thing.

And here's the thing, Pope Francis:
You need this. You need us.

Love,
Cassie

PS
My birth name is Mary. She co-created
this poem with me and my friends, too.

PPS
We look forward to hearing back from you!

Co-Created with Katherine Mancuso, Vicky Saye Henderson, Russ Eidson,
Norma Jeane Tiner, Melinda Oliver, Al Black, Daves Here Man, Gail McGrail
Glasser, Chie Guenther, Nicole Thompson-Smith, Daniel Dowe, Kris Friend,
Betty Cobb Gurnell, Worthy Branson Evans, Janeen Musselman, Amy
Coquillard, Bahiyyih Young, Zoe Viveca Sumner, Amy Alley, Debbie Turner,
Betty McCoy, Cindy Patterson, Elizabeth Wilder Platts, Mary Ann Joseph, Leisa
Marie Mounts, Barbie Smith Mathis, Barbara H Thomson, Blanche Premo-
Hopkins, Laura Gaffke, Alison Beard, Tammy Wilkins Jenkins, Helen Summer,
Susanne Kappler, Libby Bussinah, Lisa Nielsen, Caroline Flow,
Abstractalexandra Artist, Casey Catherine Moore

April

The Birth Song of Seasons

For those born in Spring,
life is a ridiculous Yes,
each day a pregnant jewel,
capacious with blessings.
Even the rain is miraculous.

Summer births in golden light,
a glow shines even in uncertainty
and emotion heals a broken heart.
Their miracle herbal cream soothes
even the rigid, turns the doubtful serene.

Autumn has a confounding partner
who sings, Yeah, Baby, whatever, don't stress,
misguided is my middle name!
Let me turn your oedipal perineal in the rain!
We can unite, an oxymoron of the blessed!

Winter babies wrestle with the ecclesial,
and waver between prediction and grief.
When rain falls, they try to measure it.
In old age, they learn to accept it, and are
showered with blessings of snow and belief.

Co-Created with Doug Graul, Robin Zavada, Elaine Murray, Ann Poling, Leisa Marie Mounts, Katherine Beth LaPrad, Amy Alley, Christi Stewart, Kris Friend, Tracey Waters, Laurel Posey, Stacey Hamilton, Annie Hitselberger Fell, Jessica Leigh Wells, Daniel Dowe, Lizbeth Finn-Arnold, Lisa Nielsen, Kezia Slaughter, Bonnie Goldberg, Olivia Anderson, Julianna Temple-Roberts, Grace Pickens Burns, Mary Ann Joseph, Al Black, Rebecca C Jacobson, Louise M Greer, Casey Catherine Moore, Cara Holman, Betty Cobb Gurnell, Elizabeth Akin Stelling, Oma Boyd, Duna Miller, Karen Fuchs

Born in April, in the 60s

This country used to have an aspiration.
Even here, in the south, we believed in the pinwheel
of freedom. Everybody had a chance.
We were all dandelions. We could sprout up
in every yard. It might have taken CPR. The nightly news
brought intrigue. We could have, against a backdrop of
drums, been free. All it took was passion.
And for the gay and literary, onomatopoeia.
Then brought April and taxes, daddies yelling
in jammies over budgets and axes. Damn.
For a second our nation was cozy and celebrated.
Then came the swashbuckling Tuesday commentators.
Lunch comes on Wednesday and there is joy. Shit switches.
Our heart imagines a boy. We are smooching, bedazzled.
This could be a dream. It could be Barack, or Fabbio, or the one
that got away, or the husband that we have never truly seen.
This is what freedom means—from the 60s to now.
Joy. Imagination. Creation. All the words your smooching ancestors
saw more clearly than you when they lay down to make you, but could not
spell the words to get to you now. Imagine it. Create it.
Feel the joy. Everything you want for your life and can have it now, what are you
waiting for. Bedazzled Boy. Obsession Girl. Go get it.
They have been waiting for you all this time to go get it.

Co-Created with Annmarie Lockhart, Cara Holman, Rebecca C Jacobson, Coralee
Harris, Ann Poling, Louise M Greer, Fredric Mau, Chris Carney, Janeen Musselman,
Libby Bussinah, Jeanette Gallagher, Jeannie Pickett Eidson, Kendal Turner

Our Whole Human Life

I am awake after a night of vivid slumber,
internal dreams where I watch a cobra
transform to a hawk and take flight.
I am ready for a day of celebration.
I start with coffee in tranquil morning
light. Gifts surround me—from my mother,
sister, and a soul friend. I prosper.
Lunch later with girlfriends, avocado
salad, sex talk, and laughter.
Lovecake with the family at dinner.
Later, my dream, like a radiant beacon,
will beckon me back to bed to celebrate
further in my head when this day is over,
and I imagine our whole human life
is meant be spent like this: halfway
between cobra and hawk, walking days
of joy and flying nights of transformation.

Co-Created with Alissa McElreath, Coralee Harris, Clint Wills, Corey Mesler,
Christopher Allen, Janeen Musselman, Holly A Sieuleaux, Virginia J Pulver, Lisa
Nielsen, Charlotte Koon Ehney, Rebecca C Jacobson, Annie Hitselberger Fell,
Anne Nichols Miller, Kezia Slaughter, Mary Hutchins Harris, Mildred Speidel

The Sky Speaks to You

I am calling a moratorium on cerulean.
Serfdom ended long ago, I think we can
conjure new words for blue, don't you?

Come walking with me on a technicolor
journey. Let's start at dawn, with the mystery
of the way lavender spreads and moves along.

Then enter the grace of mid-morning, the clarity
of me that even clouds hide from. This is the color
of wanting to whistle and touch and tap and hum.

Mid-day, my mood becomes reticent. This is a shy
blue, when the sun tends to discombobulate all
my plans, except for one cold gelato in your hand.

Then comes my rain. It is my way of quieting
the lovable cacophony of wordy noise you make.
I love you, but even the sky needs an iota of a break.

And when I clear, the watercolor festival begins.
I paint pomegranates, strawberries, and blossoms
in the wind, dancing, zumbalicious, in their skin.

When day ends, I seem to disappear into horizon.
This is the rise of belief, human. I am still there, in
dark air. In serendipitous dreams, I caress your hair.

Co-Created with Robin Zavada, Lisa Nielsen, Tina Taylor Newton, Bonnie Goldberg, Trish Vicino, Daniel Dowe, Ellen Kline McLeod, Feili Tu, Kezia Slaughter, Tamela Spires Hastie, Mary Sternick Brock, Copeland Kapp, Sandy Mau, Kendal Turner, Veronica Dangerfield, Louise M Greer, Joyce Norman, Nicole Thompson-Smith, Laura Gaffke, Leisa Marie Mounts, Lisa Gornicki Bolender, Bonnie Goldberg, Elizabeth Akin Stelling, Olivia Anderson, Gail McGrail Glasser, Marguerite O'Brien

Mother Fluxus, or 10 Principles I Would Give My Son for a Creative Life

1. Simplify for phenomenal contentment.
2. Justice blooms like a rose from disappointment.
3. After the age of 12, resist most urges for playoffs and sweat.
4. Breathe the harmonious balance of give and get.
5. Give tearful sugar and a wink to those in mourning.
6. Stay ambulatory during juggernauts and zipper schwing.
7. Increase the allure of your surroundings with an aromatic candle.
8. Greet the grumpy with talk over a grill that you enkindle.
9. A sock is not meant to be worn until the contents are alluvial.
10 Pause for a while every spring, for dogwoods are incredible.

Co-Created with Laura Gaffke, Coralee Harris, Bonnie Goldberg, Marguerite O'Brien, Kezia Slaughter, Grace Pickens Burns, Kathy Paget, Daniel Dowe, Lisa De Santis, Casey Catherine Moore, Tina Taylor Newton, Elizabeth Akin Stelling, Carla Blankenship Mangine, Christi Stewart, Kendal Turner, Tamela Spires Hastie, Doug Graul, Steve Hait, Lisa Nielsen, Sandy Mau, Diane Hare, Veronica Dangerfield, Louise M Greer, Mary Sternick Brock, Lisa Gornicki Bolender, Trish Vicino, Kris Friend, Cara Holman, Katherine Beth LaPrad

The Heart and Head and History and Hunger

One night in New Jersey, in a Prius
passenger seat, I sensed a sudden pulsing
heat in my heart. It gave me a start and

I thought, "This must be what my mother
means when she says she feels her
pacemaker make a clack," and then a

whoosh went from my chest to head,
I couldn't hear a thing, and I remember
thinking, "Soon I might be dead."

And then the discord on the radio came back
and I thought, "I must tell my driving friend
what just happened," but I waited for her story

of lust and liberty to end before I broke the
news of my recent history and how this
experience was something to surpass

even the most terrifying stories that we have
seen on screens while eating popcorn and candy
and then resume racing about the town.

"It's just low blood sugar," she said, reducing
my near-death encounter to mere falderal.
"Let's eat and you'll be fine and dandy."

I let go of my vision of a death dance
and an ambulance and phone calls to my family,
and for the millionth time (in this life, anyway),

I gave up, gave in, and admitted I was helpless.
My mother used to cook us parsnips
at Christmas, and I have loved them ever since.

My husband hates them, says they're bitter,
need too much salt and butter to be palatable,
and that is not good for his heart.

Here is the important part I have learned about
the heart and head and history and hunger:
these take a lot of time. You must be willing

to surrender. You must take the time to linger.
You must cook these things as long and hard as
they require—years!—for them to have pizzazz.

Co-Created with Clint Wills, Betty Cobb Gurnell, Virginia Clare Andrews, Rebecca C Jacobson, Bonnie Goldberg, Annmarie Lockhart, Christine Sahli Helms, Kezia Slaughter, Wendy Zhang, Julianna Temple-Roberts, Ray Sharp, Amy Coquillard, Janeen Musselman, Zoe Pruitt Owen, Daniel Dowe, Lisa Nielsen, Libby Bernardin, Duna Miller, Kimberley Goeglein Puryear, Corey Mesler, Stacey Hamilton, Charlotte Koon Ehney, Kate Fox

Cassie Premo Steele

The Irony of Autonomy

We are never really free.
At the primal level, we need
a seed to make all beings
from a baby to a weed.
Even curry needs a mix
of hot and sweet. We need
wings to fly, and gardeners
know that day turns into
night. Every freedom is
timely in this way.
Pulsation needs a wave.
Ricochet needs a place
from which it came.
We think freedom is
being unrestrained.
But even love, like rain,
combines the tense restraint
of petrichor with the sweet
release of downpour.
Autonomy is a matter of
authenticity, being from the core.
We read the holy words,
but we know their power
is not contained in the phylactery.
We pray for dunamis,
but we know that it is
through connection, bond
and transformation, energy
and deep relation that we change.

Co-Created with Virginia J Pulver, Candi Padgett, Robin Zavada, Tamela Spires Hastie, Grace Pickens Burns, Christi Stewart, Kezia Slaughter, Bonnie Goldberg, Karen Fuchs, Al Black, Lisa Nielsen, Gail McGrail Glasser, Julianna Temple-Roberts, Feili Tu, Roy Vasey, Zoe Pruitt Owen

90

Friends for Life

I often wake from sleep with disappointment.
I wanted renewal. But what I got was veritable
graffiti in my mind. Do you do this?

Sometimes I absolutely think I want a kiss.
But instead of an extraordinary unfolding
of bliss, I get a little forgiveness. You, this?

I envision my hearth lit with illumination.
Then the contractor comes and I am hit
with a bill of excruciating recalibration.

You say I am prescient? You say you, too,
have made such an adjustment? You
thought you were marrying frisky and

he turned reactionary? You tried to sow
peace and settled for tenacity? You
wore an ostentatious fabric and instead

of courage, you prayed for invisibility?
You tried to cook burgoo and ended up
with warm flippers on your plate?

Relax, my companion in skewed perception,
I will not try to placate. I will not bore you
with a cacophony of "Be grateful." Blah!

The word phony is hidden in that optimistic
sorry swill. You will not swallow it. Nor will
I. I will just say this: **Persist!** If you will, I will.

This will be our commitment. Friends for life,
pissed at what much of life gives us. Not easy
to forgive. But still we persist. Now let's kiss.

Co-Created with Trish Vicino, Annmarie Lockhart, Carla Blankenship Mangine,
Kendal Turner, Liz Cunningham Delp, Veronica Dangerfield, Daniel Dowe,
Pamela Cauthen Meriwether, Leisa Marie Mounts, Casey Catherine Moore,
Mary Ann Joseph, Cathi Christmus, Kathy Paget, Gail McGrail Glasser, Louise
M Greer, Joyce Norman, Debbie Turner, Renee Bergeron, Kris Friend, Elizabeth
Seay Cameron, Gianluca D'Elia, Jeanene Ogburn Sink, Nicole Thompson-
Smith, Tina Taylor Newton, Steve Hait, Janeen Musselman, Kezia Slaughter,
Grace Pickens Burns, Jeannie Pickett Eidson, Marguerite O'Brien, Ellen Parker
Dukes, Kimberley Goeglein Puryear, Mildred Speidel

Tale of Two Vals

I have two Vals in my life. The first is
a psychic who longs for a wife. The other
sits on an Atlantic teal island escaping
the poltergeist. Both are finally finding
ways to breathe. I tell their tales today
so you, in your life, can gain some ease.

Before Val 1 returned to the delicious
river of her youth, she was maudlin, and
rarely saw the sun. She survived eviction.
She worked overtime, even on holidays,
but never came to desired fulmination.

Val 2 went to the middle of the ocean
to escape the flood. The rain continued
for months, and yet she waited for the
glitter rainbow that did not come.

It took Noah 40 days, but the Vals
needed 53. They are women, and
quite dichotomous in their bulbous
anatomy and their relationship to
the Almighty. They didn't build a
boat, you see. They moved to Inuvik
to have a flat land where they could
expand and be. So can we. So can. We.

There they found a comrade. The first
Val chose a calico, and together they
created a fiesta with a newborn mouse.

Elton John sang to them, they danced
and drank and laughed and cried in
every room of that crow nest house.

The second Val needed a fresh place
to go. It was cold. It was the opposite
of musical and frolic, and, all alone,
the world wide web became her hope.
From that winter island, her avatar sent
out the truth of pain and starve that
women ate like beams of sunshine
until they were belly full and glowed.

And here is where the wheel of the day
turns as it makes its way: the Vals stayed
faithful. Not in a wife and Mary-Martha
kind of way. More like Magdalene, that
rambunctious ball of sin who rolled the
stone away. You, too, can do this today.

Take your nudiustertian dreams from
the day before yesterday. Pack them on
your back and go away. Find a comrade
on your path and play. Open yourself
to work and flood and land and laugh.
Open to cold and alone and a hungry
belly begging for hope. Forsake the older

vow and stale joke. Refuse any longer to
choke. And from this Val place within,
feel the soft violet beginning to spin.
In this way, we can win. We can. Win.

Co-Created with Lisa Nielsen, Mike Amason, Meg Haworth, Sandrine Dupon, Russ
Eidson, Bahiyyih Young, Katherine Mancuso, Virginia Lee Pfaehler, Wendy Zhang,
Anastasia Shaw, Scott West, Jeanette Cheezum, Kathryn Van Aernum, Kate Fox,
Casey Catherine Moore, Natalie Brown, Rachel Lucas Muckenfuss, Christine Marie
Beasley, Feili Tu-Keefner, Faith Mathis, Robert Lewis, Elizabeth JoAnn Sumner Jones,
Susanne Kappler, Cheryl Anne Cudmore, Mildred Speidel, Joyce Norman, Coralee
Harris, Mary Hutchins Harris, Chie Guenther, Tammy Wilkins Jenkins, Kris Friend,
Sarah Harrington Cross, James J Lundy Jr, Barbara H Thomson, Laura Gaffke, Betty
McCoy, Gail McGrail Glasser, Al Black, Caroline Flow

May

After a Night in the Garden

For a short time last night I held a vigil.
The stupendous storm, its thunder rattle
and rapid lightning flashes, kept me
awake. To hold up the night can be most
rewarding. To unwind the clockwork
of the working world and transplant
your thoughts and wishes in a darkened
field: my sister's baby, our limping
bunny, the earth and money and all the
soldiers fighting, wherever they may
be. So much we cannot see, cannot
control or know, but must be content
with a lightning flash of hope, a rain of
courage to be kind, and when the pain
gets bad, a thundered moment of
relief. Summer can be the hardest season
and it has just begun. I went back to bed
humming a requiem for all I had not done,
and prayed for peace. In the morning,
the squash vines looked like waterlilies
in the garden. How they had grown!
We all need water when we are feeling
testy or afraid or alone. It is what distinguishes
us—human, plant, and animal—from stone.

Co-Created with Daniel Dowe, Coralee Harris, Kezia Slaughter, Janet Hull,
Gail McGrail Glasser, Charlotte Koon Ehney, Amy Coquillard, Rebecca C
Jacobson, Bonnie Goldberg, Betty Cobb Gurnell, Elizabeth Akin Stelling

Oprah Under the Poetry Tree in 25 Scenes

1.
She: "It is never the child's fault."
Me: "I begin my healing from assault."

2.
She: "What is most important is what is true."
Me: "How do I discover, mother, what it means to be you?"

3.
She: "The closet will swing open just a crack."
Me: "I am watching and learning how to have my own back."

4.
She: "Your inner beauty is an orchid."
Me: "I forgive myself for what I did."

5.
She: "Your soul is indelible."
Me: "I am able."

6.
She: "What you do from deep in your heart is enduring."
Me: "I see my writing as a form of curing."

7.
She: "Being different is courageous and charismatic."
Me: "I am bringing down old secrets from the attic."

8.
She: "Largesse is not about your dress size."
Me: "Starving myself is never wise."

9.
She: "You must read *Where and When I Enter*."
Me: "I have found my mentor."

10.
She: "Enjoy this delicious pudding!!!"
Me: "Hunger is not a matter of shoulding."

11.
She: "Wear this new fashion!!!!"
Me: "It doesn't fit. Let's get back to compassion."

12.
She   "We're going into the homes of the filthy rich!!!"
Me: "Watch it, girlfriend. You do not have to scratch every itch."

13.
She: "My mission has been questioned."
Me: "That's more like it. Now the fruit you bear has ripened."

14.
She: "Nation, on the question of race, it is time to use your brain."
Me: "Yes. This is making bread from grain."

15.
She: "You can create a whole and happy life from what is in your soul."
Me: "I am learning to let go of control."

16.
She: "Book clubs are so awesome!"
Me: "What is awesome is what is in us that books blossom."

17.
She: "Being here now is authentic."
Me: "Reality TV meets my personal mystic."

18.
She: "Justice is exponential."
Me: "Color, class, and gender are not the limit of our potential."

19.
She: "Obama is my dude!"
Me: "Politics meets poetic étude."

20.
She: "We have the power to change a nation."
Me: "We did what you said and voted YES to inspiration."

21.
She: "The unlimited potential of your influence is in you."
Me: "I am alive to all that I can do."

22.
She: "I think Jamie Foxx and Will Smith are swarthy."
Me: "There's no place like home, Dorothy."

23.
She: "Here's a great big bunch of awesome stuff for free!"
Me: "Can I borrow your oak tree?"

24.
She: "You are what matters to me."
Me: "I thank you for showing all of us what we can be."

25.
She: "And now I say farewell."
Me: "In me, Oprah, you will always dwell."

Co-Created with Karen Fuchs, Rebecca C Jacobson, Nicole Thompson-Smith, Kristine Harvtigsen, Kezia Slaughter, Kaitlin Ohlinger, Gail McGrail Glasser, Duna Miller, Sunita Dhurandhar, Sara Eaton, Alma Luz Villanueva, Grace Pickens Burns, Robin Zavada, Russ Eidson, Christine Tapson, Kimberley Goeglein Puryear, Jeannie Eidson, Christi Stewart, Lisa Nielsen, Feili Tu, Julianna Temple-Roberts, Anne Nichols Miller

Wolf Road

A wolf came to me on a magical train.
His coat was golden.
He was singing my name.
Come with me, love. Be my witness.
Learn what it means to be mobile.
Here is what I am offering. This is my gift.
There was a bridge in his voice.
It led my spirit to dream.
I went with him beyond choice.
I learned to walk on four feet.
We followed conclusion.
A map of serendipity.
His song was enduring.
Carved a circle in me.
He used his teeth with precision.
To tattoo on my skin: Believe.
He showed me microclimates.
From glacier to verdure.
Days became weeks.
We slept under the shimmer of moon.
Strangers were kind to us.
Gave us cool wine and hot soup.
I saw many miracles.
This wolf body put on a show.
A wolf paw for absolution.
A wolf eye for a glow.
A wolf coat for exhaustion.
A wolf kiss for the hiccups.
A wolf belly for stalemate.
And of course, everywhere we went,

A wolf call for hello.
We ended on the bridge in San Francisco.
He told me the story of Francis.
His friend from so long ago.
How he taught the wolf language
Of moon and flora and fauna,
The secret of traveling merry,
Sowing love wherever we go.

Co-Created with Veronica Dangerfield, Cara Holman, Leisa Marie Mounts, Daniel Dowe, Russ Eidson, Kathy Paget, Louise M Greer, Nicola Waldron, Amaryllis Turman, Gail McGrail Glasser, Kris Friend, Cindy Patterson, Katherine Beth LaPrad, Tamela Spires Hastie, Coralee Harris, Copeland Kapp, Debbie Turner, Annmarie Lockhart, Jeanene Ogburn Sink, Pamela Cauthen Meriwether, Ellen Parker Dukes, Kate Fox, Kezia Slaughter, Mary Ann Joseph, Southcarolina Artists, Joyce Norman, Lisa Nielsen, Audrey Horton Shifflett, Betty Cobb Gurnell, Marguerite O'Brien

What the River Guide Said

What will we see on our trip?

All species are in flux.
It depends upon the moon
and her soulful pull on us.

How long have you done this?

I got my badge years ago.
I am grateful to my brother.
Without him, I might have given up.

Surrender. I know it. Why did you resist?

The nuance of the light on water,
the way it plays with shadows
on the land. The way it cuts.

It's getting dark here, like an abyss.

But see the lovely poplar tree,
reclaiming what is on the shore,
turning it to yellow flower leaves.

Do you hear that hiss?

Look where the currents ripple
and begin to twist. Just beyond
it is the nest of the river badger.

The branches of these trees are prickly.

Hold still. You won't be disappointed.
See how the lyrebird on the bank
mimics the action of another species.

It's as if their roles are introverted.

Don't you mean inverted?

Call me Malaprop.

You're funny. Stop. Don't blush.

I can't help it. In nature, I feel dumb.
Words are my riversong. How I hum.

That is no blemish. I'm not a book chum.
It's why I started running rivers like a fish.
I guess it's kind of boyish. Step out now. Steady.

The ride is done? Already?

That's it. Good fun.

You've got another run?

All day, every day.
Goodbye, dear one.

Co-Created with Tracy Gould Sheinin, Mary Sternick Brock, Kezia Slaughter, Elizabeth Akin Stelling, Elaine Murray, Diane Charuhas Gould, Louise M Greer, Nicole Thompson-Smith, Daniel Dowe, Kris Friend, Gail McGrail Glasser, Bruce Clark, Jeannie Pickett Eidson, Grace Pickens Burns

The First Shower

The first shower I had after my daughter slithered
from my body was a circle of baptism for me.
My body, like pasta in the colander, hot and wet
and new, rearranged in the water with the knowledge
of what I could do. I was clean like a pinky china
cup. I brewed the tea of mothering success and
drank it up. But twelve years of tea pots is a lot.
Tannins collect on the bottom. The water goes
cold. Each swallow has the ubiquitous taste of
the other one. Be alarmed if you must, but
mothering gets old. My daughter hardly needs
me now. I am broken-hearted and long to be
undone. I want the lush water of that first shower,
a scream in the library, the song of something new
to come. Some women take a lover in times like this.
It is not sex they are after, it is their own desire
they want to open, wrapped in paper with a bow.
Their own bodies surprising them under fresh lips,
their skin a new field, seeds in hand, ready to
sow. And when rain comes and waters the earth,
those seeds will have their own first shower,
a blessing and promise that something can grow.

Co-Created with Kris Friend, Kate Fox, Gail McGrail Glasser, Cindy Patterson,
Katherine Beth LaPrad, Diane Hare, Trish Vicino, Tamela Spires Hastie, Louise
M Greer, Veronica Dangerfield, Cheryl Thomas

What I Learned From the Angels

Not all music is hopeful. We surely sing the blues.
You, human, can stretch only so much in joyous
excess. We've seen you, in innocent anticipation,
lose. We feel the pressure of knowing the radiance
of human essence. But we admit thirsty, sleepy people
challenge us to ask for assistance. When there is
glitter in the rain, we know you are sad and we are
close by. When you are jovial, we place a glimmer
in the feline eye. We traipse, cherubic, on guitar strings
of temerity, as we teach you to fly. Three is the count
of sacred repetition. Diamonds are not priceless. Peace
is not only in heaven. It is not a miracle to be clairvoyant.
You just have to know the right recipe for sugar-pie.

Co-Created with Kendal Turner, Kris Friend, Al Black, Duna Miller, Amaryllis
Turman, Lisa Nielsen, Stacey Hamilton, Gail McGrail Glasser, Grace Pickens
Burns, Carrie Young, Ellen Parker Dukes, Joyce Norman, Gary Johnston, Louise
M Greer, Elizabeth Akin Stelling, Tina Taylor Newton, Cindy Patterson, Elaine
Murray, Carla Blankenship Mangine, Cara Holman, Trish Vicino, Susan Lenz,
Russ Eidson, Hotep Amir, Charlotte Koon Ehney, Liz Cunningham Delp, Cheryl
Thomas, Carol Agnew Black, Jeanette Gallagher, Lisa Gornicki Bolender

Euphoria Is a Word With Secrets

Cowgirl has ow.
Put a bandage on that, girl.
Command has com all over it.
Wipe it up.
Time holds Tim inside.
Leave him.
Gossamer hides same inside.
So boring.
Orchestral has a chest.
Open it up.
Dew has ew.
Clean that up, too.
Tickets get you into tic.
Pull it out.
Fox has an ox.
Let him carry you.
Bubbles have a bub.
Give him a drink.
Twist has an is in it.
Just be.
Plunge carries a lung.
Sing it, just how you want it to be.
Emotional is easy.
Motion is all you need.
Lighthouse is the light
That sets you free.
Yee ha! is a cry of glee.
Nothing hidden in there.
Let go of the secrets.
Layers hold within them lay.
Lie down in liberty.

Co-Created with Joyce Norman, Robert CJ Graves, Lisa Nielsen, Cara Holman, Ellen Parker Dukes, Michael Tweed, Casey Catherine Moore, Liz Cunningham Delp, Russ Eidson, Kendal Turner, Carla Blankenship Mangine, Suzanne Kamata, Jeanene Ogburn Sink, Elaine Murray, Kezia Slaughter, Annmarie Lockhart

On JK Rowling's Commencement Speech to Harvard

The Facebook movie was mostly hyperbole:
they exaggerated the depth of college friendship.

Harvard grads might be expecting glory:
they have been sated with esteem at every meal.

(It has fewer calories than cake and ice cream
and keeps you looking like a beanpole.)

But today I give you in poetry the essence of
what a widely shared mobile video link can deal

(but as you are likely sitting at your desk at work,
it may be too loud and lead to your boss's heel.)

The irony is that such failure might precipitate
the compost from which true success can arise.

(For even JK Rowling cannot memorize: she had to read
each word of her Harvard speech to the crowd.)

In it, she said that life is like a rodeo: Hold on tight,
not to grades, awards, or accolades.

(I take poetic license here; in her gracious discourse
sweaty cowboys in leather chaps never did appear).

Instead hold to the grace and clarity and insight
that come with surviving through impending night.

It is the sunshine of our empathy that we shine
on human moons: we can be encircled by the light
of true success—in faces, in books, in rooms.

Wednesday

Co-Created with Coralee Harris, Lisa Nielsen, Robin Zavada, Karen Fuchs, Kimberley Goeglein Puryear, Kezia Slaughter, Pamela Cauthen Meriwether, Gail McGrail Glasser, Caroline Hatchell, Al Black, Christine Sahli Helms, Janeen Musselman

June

The Fifth Element

We had four elements:
The earth was bustling.
There was oil in the ocean.
Fire wasn't helping.
Despair in the air.

I wanted a fifth thing there:
the quintessence of ether
to transform despair.
Humans are the essence
of not knowing

what they are doing, said the tree.
Dance joy with me then, I said to the tree.
Dogma doesn't turn me on.
It felt like midnight.
I wasn't wrong.

I was wearing saffron knickers.
Serve something succulent
was my motto.
I wanted the sanguine world
to ululate a new song.

Tomorrow would take too long.
End the hush today.
Only serious play can cleanse
this dance floor.
We turned the music on.

Co-Created with Robin Zavada, Amy Coquillard, Sunita Dhurandhar, Kristine Hartvigsen, Charlotte Koon Ehney, Suzanne Kamata, Rhonda Baker Uzzolino, Becci Robbins, Kimberley Goeglein Puryear, Christi Stewart, Stacey Hamilton, Adrienne Leeds, Katherine Beth LaPrad, Christopher Allen, Natalie Brown, Mark Plessinger, Rebecca C Jacobson, Julie Smith Turner, Cindi Boiter, Vicky Saye Henderson

Summer Is Sacred Here in the South

Summer is sacred here in the south.
Heat and humid are our words of belief.
Watermelon and mosquito are our saints;
they surrender themselves in our bodies and mouths.

Relaxation is our communion;
we eat it with clammy skin, wash it
down with sweet tea and bless it
with the persistence of monks.

Then we jump. Into the pool, the ocean,
the sprinkler, the cool of the porch.
Then we scrapbook. Then we look
as the turbulent afternoon haze

morphs into evening with thunder
and explosive light. Not much else
happens. It is sort of like reading Camus.
The young 'uns get exasperated,

whine at us in a kinetic frenzy that
there's nothing to do.
Put on a musical, says one of us.
Measure Nana's edema, says another.

The quiet one in the corner whispers,
Get on the bus. They stare at us, uncertain
of this religion, this cult.
It is not their fault.

We have lived through many summers.
Our hearts have melted and made us contrite.
We remember being young, our own unbelief.
We were all born again through this boredom and heat.

Co-Created with Anne Nichols Miller, Becci Robbins, Lisa Chiu, Betty Cobb
Gurnell, MaryAnne Farmer Tillman, Leisa Marie Mounts, Suzanne Kamata, Amy
Alley, Russ Eidson, Julianna Temple-Roberts, Feili Tu, Lisa Catherine Harper,
Elizabeth Akin Stelling, Duna Miller, Gail McGrail Glasser, Kathleen Capehart
Manley, Kezia Slaughter, Lisa Nielsen, Nicole Thompson-Smith, Kristine Hartvigsen,
Carla Blankenship Mangine, Southcarolina Artists

The Garden

The garden starts its day in a canopy of cloud
and then the sun moves in intimately with head
unbowed. The inevitable opening of lily begins,
mint rises, basil unfurls her aegis of green skins,
and the elaborate stomp of fire salamanders spins
through the grass. The resounding song of cicadas
rise last. Silence is finally demolished by noon.
The paradigm of summer paradise has no room
for circumspect silence. Afternoon ushers thunderous
storms, and worms appear like boogers in their sidewalk
forms. Trees along the creek drip with tempestuous
applause, bees return to their drinking as the day takes
pause. Human happy hour starts with hot pepper
jelly and crackers. Dinner with grouper. Dessert
with babycakes and fudge. More fudge for the slackers.
Turtles lay eggs as the moon rises. Rain has made moors
by the spent blossom irises. Stars spin like marrow
on the spine of the night. Fireflies dance to see their
own light. The day and the summer go on as they might.
The fence heartily supports wild grapes as moths take
flight. Grace is a growing, uncultivated thing.
It rises at midnight, under moonflower and owl wing.

Co-Created with Trish Vicino, Kate Fox, Carla Blankenship Mangine, Joyce
Norman, Jennifer Keyser Sanchez, Lora De La Cruz, Liz Cunningham Delp,
Vicky Saye Henderson, Tina Taylor Newton, Casey Catherine Moore, Kris
Friend, Ron Aiken, Daniel Dowe, Debbie Turner, Janet Hull, Kathy Paget,
Tamela Spires Hastie, Lisa Nielsen, Leisa Marie Mounts, Louise M Greer, Betty
Cobb Gurnell, Sarah Endo, Duna Miller, Veronica Dangerfield

Creating Is Like Praying

Creating is like praying.
You may not sit in church or mosque or temple,
        but you place your fingerprint against
        the altar tilth in benediction just the same.
Paint. Play.

Creating is like praying.
You may not be baptized in pluff mud and salt water,
        but your parched soul will go sailing
        low before rising like a crane.
Dance. Rave.

Creating is like praying.
You may be reluctant to exhale your pride
        and perplexed by what is marginalized,
        but then openness and gratitude take the reins.
Write. Say.

Creating is like praying.
You may not know the ritual for Japanese tea
        and find the pomade of a preacher yucky,
        but insulation gives way to amazing entropy.
Sculpt. Shape.

Creating is like praying.
You may judge the bronchial encyclical cockamamie,
        and abhor the nimble stealth of judicial stymie,
        but huckleberry fruit comes from a heartbroken tree.
Sing. Sway.

Creating is like praying.
You may perch upon the branch and fear jumping
         into the whirlpool of sin, but one day you will
         dive, spectacular and fearless, and just begin.
Act. Direct. Dream. Teach. Pave the way.

Co-Created with Annmarie Lockhart, Christopher Allen, Lisa Nielsen, Ellen
Parker Dukes, Louise M Greer, Janeen Musselman, Debbie Turner, Betty Cobb
Gurnell, Jeff Worcester, Mary Sternick Brock, Mary Ann Joseph, Marguerite
O'Brien, Lisa Gornicki Bolender, Rachel Lucas Muckenfuss, Kathy Paget, Trish
Vicino, Joyce Norman, Kris Friend, Grant Glace Adams, Sandrine Dupon,
Nicole Thompson-Smith, Paul Mount, Tina Taylor Newton, Gail McGrail
Glasser, Tamela Spires Hastie, Cindy Patterson, Duna Miller, Virginia Clare
Andrews, Leisa Marie Mounts, Steve Hait

What Blossomed

He wheedled his way into my heart

and planted
a seed as small as an eyelash

that blossomed into bliss,
                              twenty years of cheers

each evening,
                one long life of good repair

where each heart beat
                        was there, was there, was
there,
                        reminding us to
rediscover
                each other, each other, each other
where
        we lived.

                Today in the hospital,
we laughed like we had mojitos,
our sounds explosive
                        behind our private curtain,

gathering stares
                from the lackadaisical staff and security guards.

                        We told stories about our gosling,
                who was at her Nana's,
        we had hope,
    every reason to be optimistic,
planned for flight,

and maybe another superb dinner out that night.

But no.

"¡El pueblo unido, jamás será vencido!"

And the heart,
                its blood,   once united,
                                        will never be defeated.

                                                                It spurted,
reaching out for me.

The male nurse held it
        ("hemotoma, radial artery, 911, pressure, if this happens at home")

                sharing his blood in that moment with me,

not too late.

We came home in the early evening light,
                                        exhausted.

The yellow sunflower
outside the window
                blooming in its bliss   was

still there,   still there,   still there.

Co-Created with Julianna Temple-Roberts, Daniel Dowe, Grace Pickens Burns, Betty Cobb Gurnell, Annmarie Lockhart, Kezia Slaughter, Amy Alley, Kristine Hartvigsen, Stacey Hamilton, Duna Miller, Mildred Speidel, Sunita Dhurandhar, Kimberley Goeglein Puryear, Lydia Cortes, Al Black, Bonnie Goldberg, Kathy Paget

Venus Takes a Road Trip

Eight years ago, she felt a similar emptiness.
The vibe was lost, the groove was tossed,
she was overtaken with a desire for fresh air.
She needed to move. Grapes could not quench
her thirst, not even when turned to jelly or
wine. It was like she was stuck in a greenhouse
or Cleveland. She donned a merkin and kilt,
threw her mélange in a trunk, and drove off
in a huff of triumph. She made good time.
In 2004, Venus took a road trip, got a busted
lip, but her mind had finally caught a grip.
Transits are meant to be temporary blips.

Yesterday she woke like a lotus, stuck in the
muck, with an impish desire to swing from a
trapeze. She was a narwhal with no point, an
opera singer with aphonia, she needed attention—
this she could see with clarity. So she left.
Science calls it transecting— wandering to
count what you find. Aristotle started it—
peripatetic strolling to discover the mind.
Her forte is leaving things behind. In 2012,
Venus took a road trip, played for a while on
a merchant ship, but came back to the crib.
Journeys are meant to be momentary blips.

Her next trip won't be for a hundred and five years.
That's a long time to live. Plenty of play in the limb,
shenanigans to skim, whimsical flying to forgive and
delicious chow chow to give. But eventually the lights
will dim. In 2117, Venus will take a road trip, but fear not—
she'll be back on the flip side. Love, like life itself, is
just a passing blip—crossing and tour, outing and ride.

Co-Created with Cara Holman, Paula Hampton, Shannon Elizabeth Staley, Joyce Norman, Stacey Hamilton, Al Black, Kris Friend, Elaine Murray, Lisa Nielsen, Steve Hait, Tamela Spires Hastie, Gail McGrail Glasser, Diane Hare, Louise M Greer, Mary Ann Joseph, Jennifer Smith Dearing, Bruce Clark, Kate Hammerich, Daniel Dowe, Cindy Patterson, Trish Vicino, Libby Bussinah, Amy Alley, Jeannie Pickett Eidson, Grant Glace Adams, Mary Anne Farmer Tillman, Jennifer Keyser Sanchez, Val Ryan, Marguerite O'Brien, Leisa Marie Mounts, Carla Blankenship Mangine

Cassie Premo Steele

Women's Olympics MMXI

Some ladies like to balance precariously
on one blistered ankle, eat nothing but yogurt,
give up the luscious, and live for the laurel.

While the world watches these women, day
after day, at their peaceful meet, let us recall
that there are, indeed, many ways to compete.

Some women obtain bliss by being the mama.
They find themselves blessed by contractions,
and later, diarrhea. They live for the drama.

Some ladies are wayward as steel. Stalwart,
living a life with an epitaph's variety, they
tally astonishingly few miles on their journey.

Then there are the women who are breathy.
They brandish scissors, crave the slick and
the swirling, give unduly praise to the flow.

Some never leave the studio. They conjure
power, cure arthritis, track when Mercury's
direct, with aught and circles and coriander.

When you see these champions, in their game of
choice, on TV and sidewalk and grocery, use
your voice: Say they inspire. Say you rejoice.

Let us not be content to watch women, every
four years. Let us daily hail them and each other,
in every city, as Olympians of female diversity.

Co-Created with Janeen Musselman, Talyaa Liera, Virginia Lee Pfaehler, Joyce Norman, Louise M Greer, Ellen Parker Dukes, Elaine Murray, Kendal Turner, Julianna Temple-Roberts, Feili Tu, Nicole Thompson-Smith, Linda Tina Maldonado, Lisa Nielsen, Annmarie Lockhart, Michael Tweed, Christine Tapson, Cheryl Thomas, Veronica Dangerfield, Casey Catherine Moore, Tammy Wilkins Jenkins, Kris Friend, Katherine Beth LaPrad, Jeff Worcester, Mary Hutchins Harris, Cindy Patterson, Ellen Kline McLeod, Jeanette Cheezum, Tamela Spires Hastie,Worthy Branson Evans, Val Ryan, B.A. Hohman, Alan Altshuld, Stan Galloway, Sharon Sullivan, Claudia Parnell Wolverton

The Evolution of a Woman

I was afraid to be anything but amiable.
Talk about politics—I was unable.
How capitalism works—unknown.

I could walk into a room with beauty.
Making harmony was my duty.
I knew the fashion every season.

Full of feeling—I was an ocean.
But in my mind—no motion.
There was a lacuna in the center of me.

One day the clouds dispersed.
I thought I'd gone from bad to worse.
Nothing worked—even in reverse.

I made friction with my every move.
It was like I lived in gum.
It was then I heard the hum.

It started soft and began to bounce.
It told me the time had come to announce.
It showed me how with froth and foam and bubble.

The evolution of a woman—letting go of image.
It happens when she gains the courage
to go from supine to divine.

Waistline to Einstein. Hemline to incline.
The only hinder is in your mind.
Now is your time to bubble and bounce and shine.

Wednesday

Co-Created with Candi Padgett, Kimberley Goeglein Puryear, Ann Poling, Annmarie Lockhart, Audrey Horton Shifflett, Charlotte Koon Ehney, Susan Klein Hawfield, Clarissa McFairy, Amaryllis Turman, Janet Hull, Oma Boyd, Kezia Slaughter, Rebecca C Jacobson, Michelle James, Gail McGrail Glasser, Kathy Paget, Duna Miller, Julianna Temple-Roberts, Lisa Nielsen

July

A Deeper Independence

We might watch a statue topple
and call it sublime development
and tell ourselves we lead the way—

America the beautiful, all light
and hope and breeze, transformative
liberty and all earth's fears allayed.

But I wish for some other shaking
up of power, a deeper independence
like the Fibonacci whorl on a flower—

Going past the periphery of the country,
no longer living like a tourist on this
land, but opening like a pinecone

to count conflicted scars upon our hands.
Refuse to graze on the cuisine of obsolete
history, fight dyspepsia at what came to be—

Let the crux of the florid problem show.
Peel back the fabrication and mutation
of the origin until tears begin to grow.

Imagine this: a whistle begins from the
bottom of a volcano, beyond all ageism
from the very source of creation—

And chuga chuga, lava begins to flow.
Engorged and activated, our emotion pours
like this from mountain to ocean shore.

At the bottom, a dogfish greets us and
promises not to eat us, and our weeping
is turned from lava into lavender and swirl—

The foundation of a glowing coral floor.
One blue ocean songbird rises and begins to sing
about a deeper independence for everything.

Co-Created with Worthy Branson Evans, Audrey Horton Shifflett, Louise M
Greer, Jennifer Keyser Sanchez, Katherine Beth LaPrad, Debbie Turner, Tammy
Wilkins Jenkins, Nicole Thompson-Smith, Tina Taylor Newton, Susanne
Kappler, Paul Mount, Elizabeth Akin Stelling, Steve Hait, Jeff Worcester, Kris
Friend, Oma Boyd, Lisa Gornicki Bolender, Alexandria Broughton Skinner,
Jeanette Gallagher, Lisa Nielsen, Stacey Hamilton, Amy Coquillard, Cindy
Patterson, Liz Cunningham Delp, Kris Underwood, Janeen Musselman, Joyce
Norman, Libby Bussinah, Daniel Dowe, Anna Howard

Freedom Is a Wildfire

Freedom can be easy.
A taco, the surf, a pyrotechnic
show, another night on earth.

It starts simple.

Freedom can be desire.
Angiodema, glyph, and clitoris,
scratch and spark, catch and release.

It tends to increase.

Freedom can be faithful.
Bayonet high, antimacassar on,
soldiering when others are gone.

Shock sets in.

Freedom can be spectacular.
A fire, the collision of forever
fueled by the essence of grief.

Boundaries begin to thin.

Freedom can be intuitive.
United inside, seeing clear,
we keep going. We persevere.

Reaching beyond loss and win.

Co-Created with Tammy Wilkins Jenkins, Joyce Norman, Stacey Hamilton, Annmarie
Lockhart, Alice Shapiro, Katherine Beth LaPrad, Julianna Temple-Roberts, Lisa Gornicki
Bolender, Worthy Branson Evans, Lisa Nielsen, Debbie Turner, Mike Amason, Daniel
Dowe, Jeff Worcester, Cindy Patterson, Kris Friend, Jeanene Ogburn Sink, Pamela
Cauthen Meriwether, Ellen Kline McLeod, Virginia Clare Andrews, Cathy Stayman, Gail
McGrail Glasser, Louise M Greer

This Is How a Revolution Starts

This is how a revolution starts:
Your heart, in the rain, a change.

One egret, in illustrious flight—
Your heart, singing at the sight—

Suspended belief, shattered grief—
Phenomenal changes come into being.

I mean the phenom, like an atom,
begins twisting. The way rain can

transform into steamy fragrance—
then become an effluence, a river—

or snow, melting, from a mountain.
I stood in rain like this once, felt

the vacancy of shadows under my skin—
as if larceny had taken place within—

an inner hug, a piquant shrug,
a spicy giving in to love and rum.

I gave a plethora of thanks to the skies—
You spend days creating, verklempt—

You give in to beauty, you are kind.
You work with nature and what you find.

You hike through mountain, river, and rain.
Your heart, it changes, and you do it again.

This is how a revolution starts:
Your heart, it changes, and you do it again.

Co-Created with Carol Agnew Black, Natalie Brown, Suzanne Kamata, Michael Tweed, Amaryllis Turman, Jeanette Gallagher, Jeanette Cheezum, Meg Haworth, Bruce Clark, Tina Taylor Newton, Casey Catherine Moore, Cindy Patterson, Louise M Greer, Susan DuPlessis, Elizabeth Akin Stelling, Joyce Norman, Paul Mount, Sara Eaton, Jeff Worcester, Carla Blankenship Mangine, Annie Hitselberger Fell, Mary Anne Farmer Tillman, Mary Ann Joseph, Betty Cobb Gurnell, Tammy Wilkins Jenkins, Kevin Newman, Al Black, Nicole Thompson-Smith, Virginia Clare Andrews, Diane Hare, Liz Cunningham Delp

Bastille Day Party

I have an idea for a gala and so I go
to the deli, hoping serendipity will show me
what to serve my guests—everything

from marshmallows and gefiltefish
to cheese and reindeer meat and yeasty dough
assault my nose—as I stand at the counter

like a wilted rose with my number,
wishing I were meditating, or at the beach,
or in a storm, anywhere my big idea

could manifest itself outside a kitchen.
It is awesome hot. The store's AC is busted.
I come home empty handed,

greet the husband reading law briefs
on antidisestablishmentarianism
in his briefs. Good grief.

I am the doppelganger of Dalloway
on this too humid day in the deep south.
I dread the guests whose essence

will fill up the house. So I go out.
The inscrutable garden hose, curled
like giant play dough on the lawn,

seems to sing a song: Hold me.
Use me. I know you are hungry.
But you need more than food

to fill this mood. Water is magical.
Let me pour some temporality
on your party. Show the guests in

through the side gate, tell them eating
will have to wait. Swing me over your head
and announce to the ladies to grab a dude

and dance the Volta. In other countries
this was a day for heads to roll. Not here.
This is summer in America. We're hot. We got soul.

Co-Created with Jennifer Eyre White, Cathy Marie Crawford, Katherine Beth
LaPrad, Kristine Hartvigsen, Rhonda Baker Uzzolino, Kimberley Goeglein
Puryear, Janeen Musselman, Alexis Osborne, Cindi Boiter, Kate Fox, Annmarie
Lockhart, Katrina Murphy, Jan Phillips Smoak, Laura Lane-Steele, Alexandria
Broughton Skinner, Karen Murphy, Pasi Laari, Julie Smith Turner, Gianluca
D'Elia, Atlanta Georgia, Feili Tu-Keefner, Jodi Barnes

Calliope Sings to America

Rhetoric is never eloquent.
Orange now means urgent.
Forget the sunset, coral reefs,
monarch wings, and Halloween.

Would Americans prefer a pagan
temple to a mosque at ground zero?
Stay tuned for the latest fluff.
I am a wordy woman, but even I

am exhausted by all this stuff.
America, it is time to give it up.
Turn off the talk shows, silence the radio,
get some relief. Come with me,

the lonely muse of hero's poetry,
as we try to rediscover our belief.
Let's walk down the street.
Ask that kid if he wants to play.

"No," he says, despondent.
"I saw a frog today. His color had gone
from green to xanthic. This planet is deadly
sick. The time to play is over."

America, is this what it means to be
a world power? Even your children
are loquacious about the end of ages?
Stick in your thumb, instead of a plum,

get oil and coal ash and a round
of antagonizing over happy hour.
Drink up. Don't think about later.
Frequent heartburn keeping you awake?

Then get up and declare a break.
Too much talk is a mistake.
Look what happens to the cicadas
after a summer of blabbering.

Look, I'm not asking you to be a turtle.
Try to be like the cardinal instead.
Chirp in gratitude when you're fed,
or to praise your woman.

Heroes are laconic. Morons are moronic.
Awesome red wings don't make you boss.
Neither does devastating loss.
Thus spoke Calliope. The muse of heroes. Not comics.

Co-Created with Alexis Osborne, Coralee Harris, Giänlucä Guðmundur
D'Elia, Tammy Wilkins Jenkins, Karen Storay, Jan Phillips Smoak, Rebecca C
Jacobson, Kimberley Goeglein Puryear, Kezia Slaughter, Katrina Murphy,
Annmarie Lockhart, Liz Lafitte, Janeen Musselman, Linda Tina Maldonado,
Daniel Dowe, Robin Zavada, Kristine Hartvigsen, Annette Luthy Lyon, Atlanta
Georgia, Kate Fox, Blanche Premo-Hopkins

The Family and the Nation

Family life can range from bliss
to streptococcus. Days of sunshine
and nights of rain, both the violent
and the gentle kind. And the magnetism
at the center has the power to pull us all in,
make us a nation, bound by endless
bickering, flipping back and forth
between the desire for cloture and
a need for peace. This is our vocation—
mother, daughter, son and father,
leader, rebel, warrior, or citizen—
to ride the turbulent wind until
we are exhausted, then tuck our
wings beneath us and sleep.
There have been many nights
I thought we'd lost it—the marriage,
our hope, the nation, our rope to sanity—
only to awaken the next glowing morning,
embarrassed at how little faith I carry.
We must remember: it is spring.
We have been married and a nation
only a relatively short time. And this
is the season of strawberries and wine.

Co-Created with Pete Cochrane, Julianna Temple-Roberts, Wilma Margono, Mildred Speidel, Gail McGrail Glasser, Daniel Dowe, Candi Padgett, Kathleen Capehart Manley, Virginia Clare Andrews, Pamela Cauthen Meriwether, Jeannie Eidson, Charlotte Koon, Lisa Nielsen, Amy Coquillard

History Is Like a Family

History is like a family.
That's a mnemonic.
Cajun came, for example,
as a gift from our rich uncle.
Peace usually comes when
the parents are helpless and
the kids are perplexed.
It often happens after a
fight. Dissidents are the teens
who stay up all night.
Democracy is ambiguous.
The majority live in darkness.
The ones who do the work—
pass, repeal, break through—
are like tired dandelions
in the evening dew. The law
is meant to oust uncertainty.
But even the magic erase board
does not always guarantee
that we will do our chores.
Then mom gets sad. Sometimes
she leaves when the house
is a colossal mess. It often
happens in autumn.
Right after the equinox.
But before the election.
They create ads for her
on the square TV. Usually
she comes back. She still
has days of aggravation.

But in spite of everything,
we share a history.
We are a family.
This is our destiny.

Co-Created with Kate Fox, Karen Fuchs, Coralee Harris, Lisa Nielsen, Amy
Alley, Grace Pickens Burns, Ellen Kline McLeod, Robin Zavada, Kezia
Slaughter, Clint Wills, Katherine Beth LaPrad, Deb Harris, Duna Miller, Casey
Catherine Moore, Laurel Posey, Kris Friend, Tina Taylor Newton

August

When Love Comes

Watching Oprah, I see a woman. She is listing
what she wants in a lover. She is 41. The list
is long. Oprah tells her, "There's only one man
in the world like that. And his name is Jesus."

When love does come, you think, he will sound
mellifluous, he will flow like honey, your dreams
will take a jitney to a land of joy. (Isn't this our
fantasy? Eat, Pray, Love. Foreign Travel. Cute Boy.)

Somehow you will hold your heart aloft and stand
apart from the past and what might break.
(Or is already broken. Liz was running from
divorce, and Jesus, well, you've had that course.)

This is my confession: I have three friends
in their forties who have recently found love.
In one case, he is married. And so is she.
In another case, he is an addict. (And I don't

mean coffee or yoga or climbing trees.)
In the third case, they live 4,751 miles
apart. (She did the math. She knows
the numbers by heart.) So here's my advice

to my love-seeking friends: Acceptance.
Whatever is malevolent in your path will rise
to meet you. I swear to you, this is the truth.
(And I have my own nefarious past as proof.)

This is the alchemy of love. This is pulchritude.
(The word means beauty and has its roots
in the magnolia, that cheeky-monkey tree of white
sweetness and blood red burrs that drop.)

So stop. Accept that love is a laughing gull
with a slipknot in his mouth. It is in his nature
to laugh at a random joke, and when he does,
he will drop the rope around your neck.

And this is the time to take your pick:
leave the noose there and it will congeal,
or untie it by pulling the one free end.
This choice is up to you, my friend.

Earth is a free will zone. But freedom
doesn't mean you have to be alone.
It also doesn't mean there's an enemy.
Repeat after me: "I have what I need."

Apply an embrocation as you say it.
Soothe what hurts you with a lotion.
If you have a debt, don't expect anyone
else to pay it. Keep repeating this incantation.

Call it out like a penguin on a dry and rocky
beach. And before you know it, what you
are missing will be within your reach.
When love comes, you will learn patience.

When love comes, you will be able to preach.
When love comes, there will be no list.
When love comes, you will be staying.
When love comes, play will conquer need.

Co-Created with Kim Lovelace McMahon, Katrina Murphy, Kezia Slaughter, Christi Stewart, Lizzie Thomas, Betty Cobb Gurnell, Rebecca C Jacobson, Kate Fox, Daniel Dowe, Julianna Temple-Roberts, Charlotte Koon Ehney, Libby Bussinah, Doug Graul, vox poetica, Karen Murphy, Kimberley Goeglein Puryear, Coralee Harris, Pasi Laari, Sunita Dhurandhar, Tammy Wilkins Jenkins

Thoughts During Meditation

Joy is a brazen expectation.
The smooch of God is a salty haven.
Life is a relentless festival.
I try to be the best at this.
Return to the breath. The breath.

I am mostly only defiant.
Eventually I am resilient.
All minds are isomorphic.
Rehash. Repeat. Life. Death.
Breath. Rest. Breath. Rest.

Some thoughts babble and
some whisper. My pajamas
barely cover my bottom.
I bounce between starlight
and autumn. Days grow crisper.

I am exhausted and moody.
A cricket mostly sings from duty.
My ears feel an echo, my hair
is a barrage of the unctuous.
Let go. Be trusting in the tangle.

God won't let you dangle.
The intersection of mystery
and fascination is serendipity.
I return to school daily to study
that angle within. End. Begin. And again.

Co-Created with Annie Hitselberger Fell, Duna Miller, Louise M Greer, Norma Jeane Tiner, Joyce Norman, Rachel Lucas Muckenfuss, Jeanee Bourque, Megan Serrano, Casey Catherine Moore, Annmarie Lockhart, Alice Shapiro, Lisa Nielsen, Hotep Amir, Katherine Beth LaPrad, Janeen Musselman, Betty Cobb Gurnell, Al Black, Tamela Spires, Daniel Dowe, Alison Beard, Lisa Rynex Ragusa, Susanne Kappler, Cindy Patterson, Steve Hait, Norma J Honaker, Kathie Turner, Barbara HThomson, Kris Friend, Marguerite O'Brien, Nicola Waldron, James Carpenter

Another Summer

Another summer sneaks by
like a crook who tries
to clarify his innocence,
like a socket missing his
bulb, like a third base man
hungry to vilify the runner.

Another summer saying goodbye.

Like a yellow butterfly flying,
a zumba dancer trying
to compensate for late
night eating, another toddler
avoiding her spankings,
a quixotic flutter of wings.

Another summer ceases to sing.

Like the banana joke become
mystical, a buckeye seedling
sprung up at a festival, like
the sound after Hiroshima,
a headache awash in regret,
refusing to be congruent.

Another summer came and went.

Like an exotic vaudeville
show with the verve to love
and then shuffle to Buffalo,
like a time-spinner on a quest

for liquidity, like a spastic
starfish and a wish on a daisy.

Another summer flew like crazy.

Like a hot dog with the blueprint
of relish at the ready, like peaceful
sisters who learn to positively relive
a loony childhood, like a brownie
in the mouth and how it produces
the grateful fluid of Finally!

Another summer ends for good.

Co-Created with Karen M Peluso, James Carpenter, Leisa Marie Mounts, Joyce Norman, Janet Hull, Anne Nichols Miller, Jennifer Smith Dearing, Marguerite O'Brien, Mary Sternick Brock, Bruce Clark, Ed Madden, Elizabeth Akin Stelling, Alison Beard, Julie McCrary, Tamela Spires Hastie, Joel Secundy, Kris Friend, Casey Catherine Moore, Amy Coquillard, Al Black, Liz Cunningham Delp, Daniel Dowe, Tina Taylor Newton, Ellen Parker Dukes, Carla Blankenship Mangine, Gary Johnston, Gail McGrail Glasser, Jennifer Keyser Sanchez, Stacey Hamilton, Alexandria Broughton Skinner, Nicole Thompson-Smith, Annmarie Lockhart, Jeanette Cheezum, Helen Losse, Lisa Nielsen, Louise M Greer

still we do not move

an earthquake yesterday,
felt by millions in a renal shape,
and then a hurricane on the way,
aiming for the same cobalt seascape.
still we do not move.

I suppose the earth finds this
lyrical in a way, the sweet tremor
from below, and for the encore,
a salubrious wet release and roll.
still we do not move.

last night we had an ache to tell the story,
once serene, over wine and carbonara,
an articulation of our humanness,
how we matter and still mean.
still we do not move.

seagulls float and can live anywhere,
(I once saw them living by a mall)
but we resist such a separation
even after dangerous vibration.
still we do not move.

today is the day in between, when we count ourselves
lucky, feel even serene, a bit of nostalgia for the
warmth and the clean. we throw time like confetti.
a violin plays and an emerald flag unfurls.
still we do not move.

Co-Created with Diane Charuhas Gould, Jessica Leigh Wells, Diane Hare, Deb Harris, Lisa Nielsen, Kezia Slaughter, Janeen Musselman, Kimberley Goeglein Puryear, Kate Fox, Amy Alley, Gail McGrail Glasser, Lizbeth Finn-Arnold, Anne Nichols Miller, Pamela Cauthen Meriwether, Courtney Tolbert, Julianna Temple-Roberts, Nicole Thompson-Smith, Duna Miller, Daniel Dowe, Karen M Peluso, Katherine Beth LaPrad, Olivia Anderson, Shannon Mcdonald, Kathy Paget, Grace Pickens Burns

The Love Song of Katrina and Isaac

Katrina was a hurricane. I mean, the girl was undulating.
She was a Leviathan, an inspiration for all who came
after, Rita would burn with respect for her, she birthed
circuses and was the standard of evaluation, yes, sir.

Isaac began as a joke on the Internet, a wet doppelganger
to the Republican revival, a feminist at heart, cutting
through the hobnob sparkle and revealing the acrimony
behind the illusion of blessed unity. Then he strengthened.

Love and history are an adaptation. Like Sherman, he
turned from a distracted NotZCon (the sopping city was
overjoyed) and moved on. He'd heard about the pralines
in the town of New Orleans, and he wanted to take a bite.

He wanted to come screaming in on her birthday, but she
still had confidence, would not abnegate her wunderbar status
to this profligate. So he began to procrastinate. He played with
his windsock a while, then started a flood in the Holy City.

Finally, she succumbed to the finesse of his anaconda. She had,
frankly, been feeling rather blah. Together they flogged what
was fallow, he took the opportunity to shake the peaches off
her tree, and she came to share her anniversary, in synchronicity.

Despite the typhoon they brought asunder, the Big Easy did not
call it a bummer, for almost nine months later, serendipity gave
them a Mardi Gras baby, loved by all, friend and foe, who, raised
on the carnival, became the first out gay president for the GOP.

Co-Created with Russ Eidson, Casey Catherine Moore, Tommy Lightfoot, Louise M Greer, Katrina Murphy, Suzanne Kamata, Jeanette Cheezum, Nancy Miller Chambers, Annmarie Lockhart, Alexandria Broughton Skinner, Philip Rowe, Diane Hare, Elaine Murray, Tammy Wilkins Jenkins, Keith Bates, Al Black, Nicole Thompson-Smith, Trish Vicino, Tina Taylor Newton, Cheryl Anne Cudmore, Meg Haworth, Barbara H Thomson, Lisa Rynex Ragusa, Cindy Patterson, Joyce Norman, Beth Moore, Amaryllis Turman, Veronica Dangerfield, Tamela Spires Hastie, Alison Beard, Janet Hull, Kris Friend, Stan Galloway, Nicola Waldron, Katherine Beth LaPrad, Daniel Dowe, Kathie Turner, Marguerite O'Brien, Mary Harwell Sayler, Bruce Clark, Karen M Peluso, Susanne Kappler, Cyndi Singletary Shull, Pamela Cauthen Meriwether

That Mom, Baby

Some moms make tacos in the kitchen.
Some moms work in a dark shark tank.
Some moms go to Paris and paint.
And some moms ride on broomsticks
and tango till late.

Some moms wander, lost in Shangri-la.
Some moms drink claret, get dizzy.
Some moms burn the turducken.
And some moms wear stiletto heels
even when it's drizzly.

Yesterday, I noticed my hairline
receding and knowing the interdependence
of moms and the moms they are breeding,
I brought the chalice to my lips and drove
77 like der Autobahn into the abyss.
Justin Bieber sang my swan song,
floating like an angel in a shower
of sparks, ablutions spreading to all

the moms in the dark.

Some moms are miserable and some moms are crazy.
Some moms make parsnips and some moms are languishing lazy.
Some moms play the musette and some moms are lonely.
The thing all moms share is their progeny feels like the only.

I will write about this later in prose. I need more sentences
to go from sophomoric to a scene with some clothes.

Suffice it to say that the withering gaze of mothers
judging each other did fade in an estrogen cloud.
That young man made it rain from 14 to 40—hell,
9 and 50 joined in—and it wasn't soggy. It was loud.
My ears are still ringing, a soft chiming thing,
whispering, "Remember this freedom. Be resolute.
All moms are my mom. Your daughters are looking
to you. Be that mom who loves who you are and
dances and jumps toward the stars in whatever you do.
And I was like baby, baby, baby, oh."

Co-Created with Tamela Spires Hastie, Elizabeth JoAnn Sumner Jones,
Caroline Flow, Kris Friend, Al Black, Cheryl Anne Cudmore, Mike Amason,
Daves Here Man, Lisa Nielsen, Gail McGrail Glasser, Clarissa McFairy, Ron
Aiken, Kate Fox, Jeff Worcester, Jeanne Porter Ashley, Charlotte Koon Ehney,
Cory Alpert, Mary Hutchins Harris, Ed Madden, Debbie Turner, Joyce Norman,
Mildred Speidel, Feili Tu-Keefner, Louise M Greer, Cindy Patterson, Barbara H
Thomson, Jeanette Cheezum, Kristi Krumnow Fuhriman, Lan Ngoc Hoang,
Libby Bussinah, Bruce Clark, Ryan Nevius, Abstractalexandra Artist, Kathy
Paget, Susanne Kappler, Marguerite O'Brien

An End of Summer Recipe

Ingredients needed:
capers
a sunshower
a kid in school
words
a lollipop

Step one: Eschew your dream of cooler weather. Abscond with what you've got.

Step two: Don't move. Look out the windowpane. Let yourself start in on that lollipop.

Step three: Have compassion for all of your selves. Think of all they forget and forgot.

Step four: Commit apostasy. Admit you no longer believe.

Step five: Time for capers. Sour after sweet. Like carbon fusion and together and vitality.

Step six: In the blue mosque in Istanbul, someone painted all the tiles with tenderness.

Step seven: Imagine God liking this.

Step eight: Imagine God wanting us to be less territorial and more mischievous.

Step nine: Imagine God without machismo.

Step ten: Imagine us without a sense of entitlement.

Bake until it's time to pick the kid up from school. Take her to the park. When the sunshower starts, tell her stories of foxes getting married and the devil's wife finally leaving him and witches making butter. Tell her about the tiles in Istanbul where you went with her father. Tell her she is free to believe anything she wants. And then reveal to her the whole bag of lollipops.

Co-Created with Coralee Harris, Karen Fuchs, Carol Agnew Black, Libby Bussinah, Alison Hill, Laura Hope-Gill, Julianna Temple-Roberts, Rebecca C Jacobson, Deb Harris, Kate Fox, Kezia Slaughter, Kimberley Goeglein Puryear, Bonnie Goldberg, Christine Tapson, Annmarie Lockhart, Duna Miller, Karla Turner, Al Black, Linda Tina Maldonado, Lisa Nielsen, Casey Catherine Moore, Elizabeth Akin Stelling, Zoe Pruitt Owen

Contemplate

The day after. The end of the road.

No more ecstatic. Tired like toad.

Sitting in ennui. Loss. What erodes.

News comes inexplicably. This heavy load.

Give up the platform. Silence the ode.

Jump from the kitchen. Fire is slowed.

Sit and eat mango. Sweet overload.

Be like the frog. Green grass is mowed.

Short words like Basho. Nothing is owed.

Co-Created with Daniel Dowe, Renee Bergeron, Virginia J Pulver, Robin Zavada, Kathleen Capehart Manley, Carol Agnew Black, Amy Coquillard, Pamela Cauthen Meriwether, Kimberley Goeglein Puryear, Karen Fuchs, Rebecca C Jacobson, Nicole Thompson-Smith, Kristine Hartvigsen, Kezia Slaughter, Kaitlin Ohlinger, Duna Miller, Sunita Dhurandhar, Sara Eaton, Alma Luz Villanueva, Grace Pickens Burns, Robin Zavada, Russ Eidson, Gail McGrail Glasser

September

What will happen at the 9/11 Memorial

The landscape will never be the same.
This is why they came. (Ten years.)

Not for the flusteration of the media
or the plethora of pundits. (99 days it burned.)

But for the unchanging nature
of what lies beneath the dirt.

(3051 children lost a parent.)
Someone will bring a picnic.

The words will come out pickled or
premo, then get sliced until intangible.

A quiet song will be sung.
(Citizens from 115 nations.)

There will be no roaring crowd.
(1714 hate crimes reported.)

No phantasmagoric light show.
(6 days the stock exchange was closed.)

Traders on their day off will trade
ephods for iPods, and take pictures.

Two hirsute grandfathers will
stand alone and melancholy.

(Bombing in Afghanistan began
in 26 days.) Mothers are so weary.

(200 funerals attended by Giuliani.)
Even sorrow is somewhat romantic.

A few teenagers will be troublesome.
One will get arrested. (Lost NYPD: 23.)

Kids are given snickerdoodles.
The music is eclectic. (Bodies found intact: 289.)

Not even the flag makes a splash this time.
(Time the towers fell: 12 seconds.)

No patriotism to astonish. (Count the wars.)
No blame to admonish. (Count the wounded.)

All this is for the archive. (Mourn all the sides.)
Count it all up, we who are, living, still here, alive.

Co-Created with Amy Alley, Tamela Spires Hastie, Trish Vicino,
Duna Miller, Tina Taylor Newton, Tammy Wilkins Jenkins, Julie Ellinger Hunt,
Kezia Slaughter, John Tudor, Deb Harris, Charlotte Koon Ehney, Clarissa
McFairy, Lisa Gornicki Bolender, Kris Friend, Julianna Temple-Roberts, Gail
McGrail Glasser, Christine Tapson, Lisa Nielsen, Pamila Lorentz, Val Ryan,
Casey Catherine Moore, Kathy Paget, Janet Hull, Linda Tina Maldonado

"What do you call this?"

Suppose this. Start with a premise.
We are at an awesome turn in the road.
Sort of like a birthday.
Sort of like a childhood.

It is time to prove your hardihood.
You can choose bemusement.
You can settle for contentment.
You can turn transparent.
Or you can be splayed on a stage
making extemporaneous remarks about freedom.

The tantalizing truth is we are all connected.
But what is livable to one,
another may not be able to swallow.

Some people need tea.
Some need a tissue.
Some swim in effervescence.
Others breathe the ephemeral.
Some are running from something.
Others are arising for the first time today.

What began with a sneeze is not finished.
It will not end till we are cosmic and breathless.
We are not here to castigate but to activate.
This will continue until we are awash in honesty.
This is called democracy.
This is called a revolution.

Co-Created with Elaine Murray, Annmarie Lockhart, Brian Slusher, Diane Hare, Lizzie Thomas, Lisa Nielsen, Ann Poling, Nathalie Gregg, Kezia Slaughter, Tamela Spires Hastie, Annie Hitselberger Fell, Tom Poland, Nicole Thompson-Smith, Sara Eaton, Grace Pickens Burns, Pamela Cauthen Meriwether, Jeannie Eidson, Anne Nichols Miller, Amaryllis Turman, Charlotte Koon Ehney, Robin Davidson Ranallo, Elizabeth Wilder Platts, Jessica Leigh Wells, Kris Friend, Patti Forehand, Katherine Beth LaPrad

Imagine, an Angel

Imagine, an angel with sandy feet
walking beneath clouds illuminating
what is hidden, the way daisies hide
behind the sun, then capitulate to rain,
and love them all the time as friends.

You, traveler, are on that road
that never ends. I have seen you
search for a panoply of empathy
and find it in your self in meditation.
There are no shortcuts to fulfillment.

No matter how languid you feel,
how much you want to vanquish
the appeal, how somber the
chances of achieving the effort,
still. Peace is coming.

And contentment. Call me loco,
say I sprinkle dorky dust in my
coco coffee latte, I will not argue.
Peace is coming to you. It tastes
like freedom. It sounds like this:

"You are no misfit. You weave
the fiber of your very life
yourself each day, by what
you do and create. You get help
at every step along the way.
It is you who are that angel."

Co-Created with Karen Fuchs, Amaryllis Turman, Annmarie Lockhart, Kathryn Van Aernum, Tammy Wilkins Jenkins, Veronica Dangerfield, Christine Tapson, Amy Alley, Kris Friend, Kimberley Goeglein Puryear, Daniel Dowe, Gail McGrail Glasser, Rebecca C Jacobson, Pamela Cauthen Meriwether, Michael E Coward, Lisa Nielsen, Southcarolina Artists, Annie Hitselberger, Bonnie Goldberg, Katherine Beth LaPrad, Kezia Slaughter, Duna Miller, Stacey Hamilton, Grace Pickens Burns

Open the Window

The truth is that life is cinnamon and savory
even when we get persnickety.

Life waits through the transliterate window
for us to stop our vibratory jocularity

and notice serendipity again.
All we have to do is see and listen.

See the shimmering blessings:
how they fly until the grok aligns.

Relief from the everyday is easy.
Just resist the congested and proud.

Innocence is the opposite of hubris.
Refuse to be numb.

Do another verb than inseminate or prostrate.
Watch the highlight on your startling faery wings.

See how you are fluttering in your rebirth.
Open the window so your soul doesn't crash.

Co-Created with Doug Graul, Deb Harris, Brian Slusher, Diane Hare, Amy
Alley, Lizzie Thomas, Coralee Harris, Tamela Spires, Christi Stewart, Annmarie
Lockhart, Steve Hait, Lizbeth Finn-Arnold, Pamela Cauthen Meriwether,
Charlotte Koon Ehney, Sandy DeBoice, Elaine Murray

A Writer's Totem

A writer's totem is the hummingbird.
Our bright red plume is our word.

Sometimes we get debilitated, filled
with rage, disgust, and vapid hatred.

Other times we're sensuous, tricky like
leprechauns and up to any challenge.

Some days our words are regurgitation,
mere floccinaucinihilipilification

(which means unimportant, for your
information). Writing is a crucible.

Writers cannot be content with cute
and freckles. We cannot be Mary,

both unblemished and also fruitful.
It is amazing what we can swallow.

We get indigestion. But then we rise
like a phoenix and begin to write again.

Co-Created with Robin Zavada, Ian Morris, Daniel Dowe, Annmarie Lockhart, Charlotte Koon Ehney, Lisa Nielsen, Diane Hare, Foster Hunter, Terri Lynn Mac McLaughlin, Linda Tina Maldonado, Ann Poling, Aaron DW White, Casey Catherine Moore, Camille Richardson, Duna Miller, Kris Friend, Susan L Wolfe, Grace Pickens Burns

How to put it into words

Inspiration is a coming in,
a hawk landing in your yard.

Stop trying so hard.
Keep your cool.

Let your totem be.
Watch how he breathes,

feathers shuffling.
Calm. Groovy.

Be noble like this.
Not every frog must be kissed.

Let silence visit.
Swim in your spirit.

You ask me how to put it
into words, such bliss.

Just sit.
See stillness

transform into flight,
a winged blessing

when the time is right.
Hold tight.

Co-Created with Christi Stewart, J. Drayton Hastie III, Jan Phillips Smoak, John Burbage, Val Ryan, Beth DeHart, Meg Haworth, Alexandria Broughton Skinner, Veronica Dangerfield, Eva Bird, Tracy Gould Sheinin, Ellen Parker Dukes, Tamela Spires Hastie, Christine Tapson, Kris Friend, Alice Shapiro, Janet Hull, Amy Coquillard, Ed Madden, Audrey Horton Shifflett, Cindy Patterson, Nancy Miller Chambers

Equinox Belief

Another day of death and starting over,
the transition between the core of summer
coming to its clandestine end, and the birth
of autumn, crunch of leaves and cool of air.

Equal day and night. Half and half. Fair is fair.

I have always loved the equanimity of this day,
the way the fortitude of one season gives itself
to the festive aspiration of the next. A time to be
reflective of what is destiny and what is really luck.

Balance books. Add it up. A buck's a buck.

To be honest, I don't believe in the existence
of an apex outside a science book. I am skeptical
of guarantees, quick fixes and clear messages
beamed subliminally from thieves and crooks.

Make your own message. Write your book.

But I do think there's something in the poetry
of satellites and stars. I believe the moon is
sometimes ravenous, eats too much, then
goes on diets and is imperfect, as we are.

Running, walking, or crawling. Far is far.

I also think we have the capability
of being illuminated every day, not just
when Jupiter aligns with Mars. I also love
the beauty of serendipity, its sudden song.

Life is crisp and short. A day is sweet and long.

I adore the way the world surprises us
with beauty, how it sings to us at night
through bullfrogs, and washes up like
sea stars onto unexpected shores.

Everything is open. There are no doors.

Co-Created with Cathy Marie Crawford, Clarissa McFairy, Betty Cobb Gurnell, Grace Pickens Burns, Charlotte Koon Ehney, Copeland Kapp, Cathi Christmus, Gail McGrail Glasser, Kezia Slaughter, Coralee Harris, Rhonda Baker Uzzolino, Tammy Wilkins Jenkins, Libby Bussinah, Rebecca C Jacobson, Kimberley Goeglein Puryear, Amsa Yoga, Annmarie Lockhart, Gianluca D'Elia, Amy Alley, Suzanne Kamata

Wednesday

The world was clean, this autumn morning, liberated from
the searing heat with gentle rains and lovingkindness.
I need to remember this, when my insatiable desire

rears her orange head again in the middle of the
week, motivated as she is to keep working or reaching
for comfort, craving wonderful wines and cheese

or Paris or peace and understanding. Pontificating can be
a kind of disease, manifesting as Facebook updates,
slogans, signs, and other symptoms of deceit.

But true endearment lies in what's beyond the screen.
Beyond the doing. Beyond labels. Beyond the deed.
The leaves along the creek are shaking with delight.

Even on a cloudy day, there is a kind of light.
Even on a Wednesday, there are people in our life.
Alive. Loving us. Wanting time with us. Jubilant!

Co-Created with Karen Fuchs, Wilma Margono, Coralee Harris, Amsa Yoga,
Kimberley Goeglein Puryear, Julie Smith Turner, Tammy Wilkins Jenkins,
Charlotte Koon Ehney, Lisa Nielsen, Alissa McElreath, Kezia Slaughter,
Christine Sahli Helms, Martha Kubota, Kristine Hartvigsen, Gina Langston
Brewer

The Autumnal Banquet

A stranger's love isn't always reliable.
It can be a teacup of vision. A thin telescope.

A fan's following isn't always fortuitous.
It can be a sweet serving of rainbows and hope.

A lover's splendor isn't always a blessing.
It can be a feast of tsunami. A desire to cope.

A nation's union isn't always auspicious.
It can be a nightcap of surrender. A slippery slope.

A mind's inspiration isn't always brilliant.
It can be a candy of craving. A caterwauling for dope.

The only real food that isn't entrapment
is the meal that is tempered by a final release.

Be like the trees that let go every autumn.
Stay in one place. Withstand drought and disease.

Love the land where you stand. Give your fruit to the birds.
Know you will last through the winter by eating your leaves.

Co-Created with Karen Fuchs, Ray Brown, Coralee Harris, Mildred Speidel, Christine Sahli Helms, Kimberley Goeglein Puryear, Mary Ann Joseph, Lisa Nielsen, Bonnie Goldberg, Tammy Wilkins Jenkins, Alexis Osborne, Janet Hull, Charlotte Koon Ehney, Copeland Kapp, Cathi Christmus, Kezia Slaughter, Julianna Temple-Roberts, Kristin Ferrara-McAngus, Grace Pickens Burns, Zoe Pruitt Owen

October

The Trick of Days

Some Wednesdays are unwarranted:
the hospital visit to see your mother,
the call about an aunt's death from
your brother, being unable to see
your sister in the mental ward during
lunch time. On these days, everything
is not fine.

And then there are days you combust:
the bank account goes belly up, the car
breaks down, your creepy uncle is in
town, your nemesis is in *The New York
Times Book Review*, and they call him
brilliant. On these days, it's hard to be
resilient.

But then come days you want to propagate:
ideas flow, beauty shows, sun shines,
no one whines, no one is late, the tax
collector calls and says they made a big
mistake, you are owed real money, come
and get it. On these days, your reality is
fantasy.

Here is the trick of days and their
justification: days never take a vacation.
They show up, they grow up, they take
our prompts and make something of them.
They take our heavy baggage and lean on it.
May we be so useful. May we wear such a
wise bonnet.

Co-Created with Lisa Nielsen, Copeland Kapp, Charlotte Koon Ehney, Elizabeth Akin Stelling, Stacey Hamilton, Coralee Harris, Nate Spears, Helen Losse, Kezia Slaughter, Christine Sahli Helms, Christine Tapson, Trish Vicino, Elizabeth Akin Stelling, Coralee Harris, Daniel Dowe, Amy Alley, Gail McGrail Glasser, Lisa Nielsen, Rebecca C Jacobson, Wendy Zhang, Jeannie Eidson, Sunita Dhurandhar, Janet Hull, Grace Pickens Burns

Some Earth Bodies

Some earth bodies grandstand.
They seesaw and handstand
but miss an essential freedom.
You see, we humans are not the
only keeper of this being. Some
earth bodies can take a field trip
to the farm but still not bring the
okra and parsnip and beans to their
own mouth with their own arms.
Some earth bodies can float in
the ocean, but remain unable to
hear the mermaid's diction.
Some earth bodies can soar
in the breeze and still be
beholden to the whisper
of friction. And some earth
bodies hold memories like
crutches and abandon hypocrisy
only posthumously. Some
earth bodies, though, have
established a heartfelt connection,
both above and below. You will
know them when you meet
them because they sound
like buzz and taste like fig.
They do not wait for drought
to let their water tables rise.
Unctuous is anathema and
anything less than blockbuster
and fabulous is not good

enough. You can see crisp
auburn leaves falling in
their eyes. They do not blink.
They see the serendipity and
know that even here earth,
we are walking with the skies.

Co-Created with Jeanee Bourque, Norma Jeane Tiner, Susan Volk, Kate Fox, Kathie Turner, Cathi Christmus, Annie Hitselberger Fell, Jeanette Gallagher, Jeanene Ogburn Sink, Louise M Greer, BA Hohman, Feili Tu-Keefner, Nancy Miller Chambers, Joyce Norman, Stacey Hamilton, Katherine Beth LaPrad, Veronica Dangerfield, Tammy Wilkins Jenkins, Cheryl Thomas, Trish Vicino, Al Black, Barbara H Thomson, Gail McGrail Glasser, Bianca Premo, Amy Coquillard, Daniel Dowe, Debbie Turner, Kris Friend, Tamela Spires Hastie, Audrey Horton Shifflett, Cindy Patterson, Lisa Rynex Ragusa, Janet Hull, Paul Mount, Rebecca C Jacobson

Conversion

My hair was wispy, but the myelin around my smile
scattered haunted whimpers that whispered fresh
pain. The phone call came. It was my mother.
Like a woodpecker at my heart was her voice.
She was in the hospital. The electric feeling
I'd been having would portend our reunion.
I went to her. "I went from twenty-five to
eighty-five," she said, as I helped her into
bed, her sachem status turned on its head,
her vibrancy depending now on what I said:
"You look great. You'll be fine. You'll be out
of here in no time." We have always led a
chiaroscuro kind of life, our family, but now
my piquant taste seemed suddenly dangerous,
a waste. I converted to agathism, there in her
hospital room, reading Thich Nhat Hanh out loud
to my mother. I was no longer searching. I was with her.

Co-Created with Julianna Temple-Roberts, Kisuri St Claire, Alexis Osborne, Kim Lovelace McMahon, Coralee Harris, Daniel Dowe, Southcarolina Artists, Amsa Yoga, Rhonda Baker Uzzolino, Kezia Slaughter, Marjorie Altman Tesser, Cathi Christmus, Wendy Zhang, Annmarie Lockhart, Stacey Hamilton, Michael Hanson, Janet Hull, Grace Pickens Burns, Lisa Nielsen, Clarissa McFairy, Robert C.J Graves, Duna Miller, Charlotte Koon Ehney, Kim Blankenship

Brilliant

I used to think I was brilliant. Then I had kids.
My daughter comes home, bombarded.
"I'll never be able to do all this," she says.
(Actually, "says" understates. Her freckles shake.)
"Let's take it one at a time," I say, thinking of those brave
souls in AA. "You're not clueless. You can do this."

She shows me the first word: infundibulum.
"I don't even know what it means!" she screams.
(Beats me, I think. My mind is blind.) "Sound it out,"
I suggest. (In fun? I wish. In fund? You jest.)
And then I feel keen: Google will know what it means!
We sit in the gossamer glow of the screen,

amazed at the infundibula in everything:
the lungs, the air we breathe, our heart, that muscle
of love, the ovary, that baby machine, even the kidney,
that bean thing, and the brain, prima causa of all this fuss—
there are infundibula running rampant throughout all of us!
How could I be a mother and still not know this stuff?

I must have spent too long napping when she did.
I should been reading something less vapid than *Newsweek*,
or been eating some super greens, or at the very least,
I should have had less to drink at book club.
I imagine this alternate estuary of my life: Me, smart as a whip.
My daughter doing her homework as fast as a flip.

Then both of us discourse on the open-endedness of body parts
and broken hearts and universal space and existential Kafka—
instead of marauding into the kitchen for another night of pasta.

We need carbs, something hardy. It looks like a long night—
late to bed, late to wake, extra coffee, another tardy.
We sit to eat. At first she only takes a nibble. I breathe deep.

(Think Zen. Just wait.) Then she opens up the gate.
In between bites of gooey cheese, she finally speaks:
there was a fight with her two best friends at recess.
It was such a mess. Guess what she said? Ooo, such hate.
I listen long. Homework can wait. I may not be brilliant,
but I am resilient, and I am teaching her this lesson, too:

There are infundibula in everyone, sublime and
open spaces in our bodies where emotion goes,
circles up into itself and grows. And everyone needs
the spiral of an open ear for what is deep inside to show.
This is how we move from gore to Gloria. This is how you reach euphoria.
It may not on tomorrow's vocabulary test, but this is what I know.

Co-Created with Cathi Christmus, Robin Zavada, Charlotte Koon Ehney, Julie E
Bloemeke, Julianna Temple-Roberts, Mary Gilkerson, Janet Hull, Kate Fox, Coralee
Harris, Kezia Slaughter, Susan Finch Stevens, Catherine Fleming Bruce, Ann Poling,
Julie Smith Turner, Stacey Hamilton, Betty Cobb Gurnell, Christopher Allen, Jessie
Carty, Alexis Osborne, Feili Tu, Natalie Brown

Metamorphosis

> "Play is the exultation of the possible."
> —Martin Buber

Start with a choice of solitude.

Some begin by becoming a boozer or giving into a mood.

We are all just students here.

Feel the confluence of that.

Meditate on the simple resilience of that fact.

You might experience a bit of transference.

Let it facilitate the transfer.

Let love take over.

Let yourself love things that fascinate.

It doesn't matter what – or who.

It could be a medieval knight, or chocolate and coffee.

Or dynamite. Or ink and glue.

Eventually this crackle will wear itself out.

You will begin to disassociate the thing from you.

Like when you hire a photographer and make an investment in boxed sets.

You start to see the art as separate from you.

You will grow laconic at this stage.

It might come from age.

Or mononucleosis.

Or an ischemic attack.

Or your mitochondria might lack some energy.

In this, you will see peace.

The old patterns become redundant.

You learn to stay on the ground like a quail.

Meanwhile, your spirit does aerial flips in the mist.

You will get used to this.

You let your body park itself on the grass.

You watch your higher, sparkly self spin in its growth.

At first, this can be hypnotic.

It happens to most.

Then it slows.

Year after year, you migrate through the seasons of you.

This is metamorphosis.

This is life. This is death.

This is human. This is planet.

This is every star and particle.

This is very old. This is how we re-new.

Co-Created with Charlotte Koon Ehney, Feili Tu-Keefner, Ellen Parker Dukes, Kate Fox, Louise M Greer, Veronica Dangerfield, Lisa Nielsen, James St John, Cathi Christmus, Al Black, Jeanette Gallagher, Suzanne Kamata, Stan Galloway, Janeen Musselman, Joyce Norman, Katherine Beth LaPrad, Amy Coquillard, Melinda Oliver, Cindy Patterson, Mildred Speidel, Gail McGrail Glasser, Kris Friend, Doug Graul, Nathalie Gregg, Debbie Turner, Julianna Temple-Roberts, Tamela Spires Hastie, Barbara H Thomson, Laura Gaffke, Karla Turner, Barbie Smith Mathis, Lisa Rynex Ragusa, Helen Summer, Pamila Lorentz, Kathie Turner, Jennifer Smith Dearing

Samhain Storm

She was undulating and her name was Sandy.
But she came with witchery instead of candy.

In Carolina, instead of crow-caw, women sang.
In this land of rice planter, we know a hurricane.

Her strength and synergy.
How quick she is and quirky.

How men yawn and kids hope.
Elders fear and mothers cope.

In the dark, the systematic destruction.
A night for burning more than pumpkin.

Through hotels, a dog swims and tuna float.
A thousand houses open doors to boats.

1500 miles was her stretch.
So far in Haiti, 58, and in tri-state, 40 deaths.

Then her withdrawal. Silence.
Survivors left wondering, What then?

H stands for haunt and hope and Halloween.
A plethora of misery NYC has seen.

A nation responds with heartfelt sympathy.
First, after 9/11, and now after the sea.

No enemy this time, except ourselves.
And here is the rainbow in this scene.

Take a breather. Commit to green.
Vote to assert our anathema of greed.

Because this is where nature is intriguing.
Both destruction and solution are in her being.

Wind, water, sun and tides and moon:
How we can transcend and heal this doom.

Co-Created with Janet Hull, Marguerite O'Brien, Al Black, Casey Catherine Moore, Susanne Kappler, Mike Amason, Kris Friend, Joyce Norman, Elyn Blackman, Cindy Patterson, Katherine Beth LaPrad, Ann Poling, Lisa Nielsen, Alison Beard, Elizabeth JoAnn Sumner Jones, Louise M Greer, Janeen Musselman, Jeanette Cheezum, Faye Kuperman, Jeanne Porter Ashley, Steve Hait, Barbara H Thomson, Beth DeHart, Zoe Viveca Sumner, Barbie Smith Mathis, Libby Bussinah, Cheryl Thomas, Pamela Cauthen Meriwether, BA Hohman

21 Ways to Respond to Mortality

1.   Get livid.
2.   Paint the positive biopsy with vivid tears.
3.   Embrace your greatest fear.
4.   Suss out an answer.
5.   Listen to your daughter's laughter.
6.   Watch the tangled become clear.
7.   Hire a dowser.
8.   Try something over-the-counter.
9.   Shed an entitlement of tears.
10. Feel the wonder.
11. Claim your power.
12. Occupy.
13. Learn to work with energy.
14. Sense time dripping by.
15. Eat a cinnamon bun.
16. Become vindicated.
17. Fast.
18. Go for a run.
19. Grasp gangly.
20. Be patient with the hopeful.
21. Love someone.

Co-Created with Jessica Leigh Wells, Corey Mesler, Kelly McKenzie Mulkins, Linda Tina Maldonado, Tammy Wilkins Jenkins, Grace Pickens Burns, Katherine Beth LaPrad, Kris Friend, Amaryllis Turman, Holly A Sieuleaux, Diane Hare, Mary Ann Joseph, Lizzie Thomas, Lisa Nielsen, Candi Padgett, Kezia Slaughter, Annie Hitselberger Fell, Karla Turner

What Death Taught Me (A Short List)

Death is not as bad as anxiety.
Your mind can be the roadkill of
Pride. You can lollygag naturally
on this journey of life, and then
Nestlé will put poison in your
baby's bottle and auto-workers
will have nowhere to hide.

Some days are like a premature
birth, senses overload and
connected love falls like leaves
to the autumnal earth. The nebula
of the mind is numb, fecundity
refuses to come, and your only
relief lies in thankful reunion.

The present is a yes.
There is no substitute, no
almost, no surfeit, no me, too.
Reconciliation is a retreat from
the pretzel of the past and a
disconnection from the impeccable
blessings of the future you.

Acceptance comes when we elect
mental illness as the honey that
sweetens an unstable plot.
Death comes to the hunter and
hunted alike, and even to those
who think they are not. Nothing
will erase what has been taught.

Co-Created with Michael Tweed, Louise M Greer, Charlotte Koon Ehney, Janet Hull, Leisa Marie Mounts, Zoe Viveca Sumner, Abstractalexandra Artist, Elizabeth JoAnn Sumner Jones, Al Black, Nicole Thompson-Smith, Daniel Dowe, Betty Cobb Gurnell, Mike Amason, Gail McGrail Glasser, Bianca Premo, Stacey Hamilton, Cindy Patterson, Kate Fox, James St John, Maria Ramsay, Alison Beard, Mary Ann Joseph, Virginia Clare Andrews, Annmarie Lockhart, Oma Boyd, Helen Summer, Audrey Horton Shifflett, Susanne Kappler, Eva Bird, Trish Vicino, Barbara H Thomson, Ed Madden, Bruce Clark, Lisa Nielsen, Joyce Norman, Feili Tu-Keefner, Lisabeth Saunders Medlock, Kathie Turner

November

Going Forward After Victory

For some, Obama means progress.
One long Hooraaaay! A yes!
Zippitty do and polished success.

For others, "Obama!" was a curse.
An herb of hallucination, and sin.
They preferred the classy jerk.

Dreams are fragile beings.
They whisper words like amitiée
And unity while blessed with hope.

And some dreams wake us to cope.
Denial ends, we admit we are screwed
And move forward at the end of a rope.

Not every day of marriage is fun.
We can be exhilarated or myopic
Or real or together or on the run.

Running a nation is like this, too.
We commit to butthurt and see it through.
We go beyond opinion and give no excuse.

And together, we open our arms and say,
You are welcome here. Come in! Hooray!
And our historic cousins let go of their grief.

We made a choice and we are the winner.
Exclusion and greed concede.
The earth sighs with relief.

We make a commitment to the world.
Every action is affirmation,
A unification flag unfurled.

So shout, "Yeah Baby!!!" and clap.
And then help your neighbor with his bootstraps.
For the changes to come are metamorphic.

We cannot be blithe. We are the phoenix.
We rose twice from the tumult
And now move forward wakefully.

We balance exuberation with work
Even as we exhale and are relieved.
True hope is acceptance in a falling leaf.

Co-Created with Carla Blankenship Mangine, Debbie Turner, Tommy Lightfoot, Cathi Christmus, Elaine Murray, Janeen Musselman, Liz Cunningham Delp, Erica B Gibson, Russ Eidson, BA Hohman, Rachel Onley, Keith Bates, Sandrine Dupon, Gail McGrail Glasser, Mary Anne Farmer Tillman, Feili Tu-Keefner, Elyn Blackman, Grace Pickens Burns, Eric L Stockard, Jeanne Porter Ashley, Ed Madden, Susan Volk, Daniel Dowe, Grant Glace Adams, Charlotte Koon Ehney, Louise M Greer, Kelly Rametta, Debra Padgett, Gabriela Lemmons, Elizabeth JoAnn Sumner Jones, Laurel Posey, Joyce Norman, Casey Catherine Moore, Lisa Nielsen, Jeannie Pickett Eidson, Ryan Nevius, Jeanee Bourque, Janet Hull, Kris Friend, Amy Alley, Bruce Clark, Marguerite O'Brien, Pamela Cauthen Meriwether, Pamila Lorentz Maria, Tamela Spires Hastie, Bianca Premo, Abstractalexandra Artist, Barbara H Thomson, Katherine Beth LaPrad, Diane Charuhas Gould

Post-Election

Now ill from the redundancy
(redo dunces dancing antsy)
and determined to do away
with doubt (out clout), I turn
off the demoralizing spout
at the center of the living room
and head to bed (be edified).

I rejoice in my dreams where
disappointing (diss this thing,
appoint that thing) election results
transform into philosophical beams
that hold up the sky (ski, cry, why).

Warily I wake in the morning
with ideas for new policy (poet,
polite, like, see) where substitution
is not an excuse for exclusion
and damp daydreams deviate
into an unchartered course
(cooperate, you, are, source).
Every wine comes from something
being crushed. Do not be baffled
(battered, awful, fled) by change.
Every river needs a bridge to cross.
Every growing thing comes from seeds
that give themselves, complete, to loss.

Co-Created with Alicia Leeke, Amy Alley, Stacey Hamilton, Betty Cobb
Gurnell, Lizzie Thomas, Christine Tapson, Bonnie Goldberg, Coralee Harris,
Kezia Slaughter, Wendy Zhang, Pamela Barnett, Tammy Wilkins Jenkins,
Julianna Temple-Roberts, Lisa Nielsen, Janet Hull, Adrienne Leeds, Christi
Stewart, Grace Pickens Burns

The Journey

There are many factors (from infection from an enterobacter
to the common cold, from severe exhaustion to lack of direction)
that can make us stop and put our lives on hold so we can start

the journey of healing from within. This is how to begin:
Start at the juxtaposition of dream and apparition
in you. The place where the Creatrix who guides the

inside you resides. She is not nice. She will defenestrate
(throw through the window) all you thought you knew.
She sucks on pomegranates and spits the pits at your lists

of things you think you should do. And when you get
melancholy, she will envelop you in stillness and call upon
your crew. "Allow me to introduce you," she says.

"Here is your angel team. The bubble popping teenage you,
the ghostly, pessimistic you, the solid you that builds a strong
foundation, the grateful you, and the you still fraught with

indecision. Let go, let crew, there is nothing more for you
to do. It's time for them to take over." So you sit and
watch: the teenager plays a ukulele and you realize how

little joy you have felt lately. The pessimist lines up your ego
and desire until they are perpendicular to your creative fire,
and the solid one says, "Build from that corner."

The grateful you says, "Bliss." And the indecisive one
blows a soul kiss and is dismissed. A chill comes over you.
You wish you could take back all the times you

hoped for something from a place of fear. But
you can't go back from here. Human is a temporal animal.
You must look forward and paddle your canoe

through this fluid of love. You get so much help
from above. Already they have planted seeds that will feed
you in the harvest season. You do not need to know the reason.

Just paddle that canoe. And keep heading toward the true.

Co-Created with Julianna Temple-Roberts, Robin Zavada, Doug Graul, Amy Alley, Mary Lynn Nash, Amsa Yoga, Jessica Leigh Wells, Trish Vicino, Diane Hare, Linda Tina Maldonado, Kezia Slaughter, Lisa Nielsen, Charlotte Koon Ehney, Tamela Spires Hastie, Natalie Alexis Osborne, Anne Nichols Miller, Duna Miller, Lizzie Thomas, Sarah Endo, Grace Pickens Burns, Annie Hitselberger Fell, Kris Friend, Jeannie Pickett Eidson, Mary Ann Joseph, Brett Sheftman, Russ Eidson

Ten Steps to Enlightenment

1. Close your eyes. See the subconscious swirl within.

2. Open your eyes. Pay attention to the vivid. Ignore the dim.

3. Avoid the pedantic and cumbersome, both stranger and kin.

4. Cultivate friendship with those who are optimistic, not spiteful.

5. Have discipline. Practice being both diligent and delightful.

6. Look into your own eyes. See your soul. Be soulful.

7. Let your birthday be a retreat day.

8. Do not run away from what scares you. Be persistent.

9. Greet the salacious with patience. Especially in your own skin.

10. Know nothing is predestined. Everything happens when you begin.

Co-Created with Jessica Leigh Wells, Gail McGrail Glasser, Kezia Slaughter, Robin Zavada, Pamela Cauthen Meriwether, Mary Ann Joseph, Lisa Nielsen, Kris Friend, Stephen Owen, Amaryllis Turman, Tamela Spires Hastie, Annmarie Lockhart, Amy Coquillard, Jeannie Eidson, Foster Hunter, Duna Miller, Charlotte Koon Ehney

Thanksgiving for Everything

Thank you, I want to say to you, full of gratitude
for all this life has given me, the blessings and
the boredom and the accidents, all three, and the
way you have taught me to move through them
with a deeper kind of insurance. You are munificent;
the gifts you bestow are echoes of a greater family,
something that belongs to everybody, some place
where everyone is included, where even fallow ground
is suited for its own purpose, where everyone works
to crystallize their talents, and serendipity is something
more than chance. We say we want to reinvent the world,
but on this day of Thanksgiving, when we sit down to pearled
onions and mashed potatoes and turkey and get stuffed, let us
say grace is something simple: the ability to be grateful for every
single thing, from the kerfuffle to the mystery of being.
Let us cook each and every moment in the brine of laughter,
knowing that next year we may not all be here, but it is this
Thanksgiving for everything we will remember for ever after.

Co-Created with Kezia Slaughter, Christine Sahli Helms, Christine Tapson,
Trish Vicino, Elizabeth Akin Stelling, Coralee Harris, Daniel Dowe, Amy Alley,
Gail McGrail Glasser, Lisa Nielsen, Rebecca C Jacobson, Wendy Zhang,
Jeannie Eidson, Sunita Dhurandhar, Janet Hull, Grace Pickens Burns

For This We Are Thankful

Cranberries, turkey, stuffing, pie.
Gathering everything.
Life.
Earth.
Sky.
One family.

Glorious health.
Sumptuous people.
Friends.
Autonomy.
Family.

Children.
Yummy food.
Self.
Love.
Family.

Touch and grace.
Blessed love.
Connection.
Community.
Family.

Love.
Life.
Sisters, brothers.
Grandsons, granddaughters.
Family.

Cranberries, turkey, stuffing, pie.
Gathering everything.
Life.
Earth.
Sky.
One family.

Co-Created with Amsa Yoga, Nelly Travez Sommerkamp, Duna Miller, Cara Holman, Jeanette Gallagher, Ellen Parker Dukes, Suzanne Kamata, Annie Fell, Kathryn Ramsby, Rebecca C Jacobson, Rachel Parker, Pamela Cauthen Meriwether, Amsa Yoga, Terri Lynn Mac McLaughlin, Jessica Leigh Wells, Casey Catherine Moore, Kezia Slaughter, Oma Boyd, Kate Fox, Betty Cobb Gurnell, Bianca Premo, Blanche Premo-Hopkins, Kris Friend, Deb Harris, Louise M Greer, Coralee Harris, Diane Hare, Lisa Nielsen, Leisa Marie Mounts

Transcend (A Thanksgiving Poem)

How to transcend
Thanks giving
Into grace:

Take an object.
Be content
With its lovely shape.

Release the willy-nilly
Of gravity and grab and get.
Be self-sufficient even

In the airport
Confusion
Of what came and went.

Be a rider
Or a righter
Or a writer.

Think of yourself
As the transcriptionist
For God.

Accept reality.
Yet be sparky.
This is your only job.

Let the meal unfold
As it will.
Compromise on peas.

Be patient with redundancy.
Your aunt's cheesecakery
Will not give you disease.

When intrigue strikes,
Put on your gloves
And clean that bitch.

The turkey may be lovely,
But grease and fire
Leave sticky bits.

Envelop the mess
In a blossom of soap.
Know the children

Are watching
How you cope.
Linger over love.

Go back to that object.
The vase, the puzzle, the tree.
This is our nation and our family.

Despite everything,
We were not conceived in hate.
Admire our lovely shape.

Co-Created with Jeanne Porter Ashley, Barbara H Thomson, Leisa Marie Mounts, Barbie Smith Mathis, Kathy Paget, Louise M Greer, Rachal Hatton, Al Black, Debbie Turner, Daniel Dowe, John Burbage, Gail McGrail Glasser, Shannon Ivey Jones, Alissa McElreath, Kris Friend, Sara Eaton, Mary Ann Joseph, Pamela Cauthen Meriwether, Robin Zavada, Annmarie Lockhart, Linda Tina Maldonado, Elizabeth JoAnn Sumner Jones, Lisa Nielsen, Janeen Musselman, Jeanee Bourque, Marguerite O'Brien, Helen Summer, Juliet Hewitt

December

What Happens in December

> "Tell me what happened, Thomas.
> Tell me what's going to happen."
> —the grandmother in Smoke Signals

While the fiddles play Joyeux Noel
in France and Haiti, light shimmers
golden over all who are waiting,
and hungry, or bored, or ready to go.

In Mexico City and Quito, Navidad
bounces out from boomboxes of long
ago. In Tokyo and Los Angeles, they
greet the season with the neon snow
of irony. Portland and Paktika burn up

with celestial incendiary. Congress
plays a piano of disarray in the
District. Last year was a year of hiccup
for the CIA and those who babble
on about traditional commitment.

All over the world, girls give up their
harrump to sing ho ho ho and forego
their glitter for one night in silence. In
Brooklyn and Jerusalem, they light

the menorah with exceptional children.
In Detroit and Dublin, they kneel
before the cross and drink until the loss
and humdrum turn out to feel euphoric.

In DaNang and Deer Park, they are
content to sit and listen to the bells
without anticipation. In Colorado and
the Mission, they see the galactic in a

dish and fear not the coming apocalypse.
In Columbia and Cincinnati, they light
up cedar and drink up cider and watch
the exaltation steam on till dawn. But

no one, in these end of days, yawned.
We did what we always do and when
the beings of love and light came through,
we were where we'd always been: here on earth,

being human, divided by faith and geography, but
exactly and perfectly filled with one hope within.

Co-Created with Al Black, Kris Friend, Janet Hull, Philip Rowe, Virginia Clare Andrews, Bruce Clark, Barbara H Thomson, Alison Beard, Susanne Kappler, Beth Moore, Pamela Cauthen Meriwether, Casey Catherine Moore, Kathie Turner, Pamela Barnett, Leisa Marie Mounts, Louise M Greer, Elizabeth JoAnn Sumner Jones, Kristi Krumnow Fuhriman, Sandy Mau, Carol Brady, Gabriela Lemmons, Barbie Smith Mathis, Helen Summer, Kristine Hartvigsen, Lan Ngoc Hoang, Susan DuPlessis, Joyce Norman, Nicole Thompson-Smith, Debbie Turner, Mildred Speidel, Gail McGrail Glasser

What I Got That Year

I got an enigma. It was boxed in silence.
It had the density of stars and carried
sadness on its back. I didn't want it.
I wasn't satisfied. I made excuses.

I thought I was having an anxiety
attack. There was frost on the window,
but my breath came so hard against
the glass that I couldn't see the great
expanse of snow. I was blinded by my
resolutions. I held myself accountable.

I thought about my career. I made vision
boards of the affluent. Success was in
another language, and I wasn't fluent,
it was somewhere far away and warm,
like a pink flamingo, which I wasn't.
And then I learned the lesson of moisture.

What looks like fog is only breath.
What cuts like ice is only water that
has learned to meditate on death.
What is cold now will be a luscious
treat on our tongues in summer heat.
All water rises and disappears.

Rain is its rebirth. After heartbreak, the sky
clears. Rivers and creeks are mellifluous
music, the sound of tears being held
by the earth while entering our ears.

What I got that year took me years
to understand. It was the gift and the
wisdom of water. How it is in me and around
me, and now, like me, it flows like victory.

Co-Created with Coralee Harris, Alissa McElreath, Daniel Dowe, Elizabeth
Akin, Jessica Leigh Wells, Ellen Parker Dukes, Kezia Slaughter, Lisa Nielsen,
Leisa Marie Mounts, Cara Holman, Kris Friend, Grace Pickens Burns, Kathy
Paget, Louise M Greer, Katherine Beth LaPrad, Kathryn Van Aernum, Annmarie
Lockhart, Marguerite O'Brien, Doug Graul, Norma Jeane Tiner

Hibernal Caves

"For even beasts and birds have memory;
else how could they not return to their dens and nests…"
—Saint Augustine

Earth and air and sun and water are coastlines,
waiting while we humans watch. My daughter
asks me what has happened, and I am crying,
and it feels like winter comes to kill what has
just hatched. I drift. I cannot keep still. I
distract myself with gifts and decorate and
switch and drive. Hibernal caves are where
we hide when we are drifting. Snow like sand
and lacy frost become our bed when we are lost.
In winter we restore. We fill our balloon for later
lifting. For now, the sun is descending. Cookies
in the oven, baking comfort. The birds are thanking
me for dinner in the dusk. Saint Francis has bare
branches around his head. Fading low is the
reverberation of wake school drive work cook
sleep and start again, that song that plays inside
my head. I pray this season teaches me to sit in silence.
I give myself a gift and declare a holiday for one hour
of silent night as dark descends upon this day.

Co-Created with Julianna Temple-Roberts, Erin Marshall Lancer, Betty Cobb
Gurnell, Daniel Dowe, Karen Fuchs, Lizzie Thomas, Robin Zavada, Virginia
Clare Andrews, Annmarie Lockhart, Alice Shapiro, Grace Pickens Burns, Kezia
Slaughter, Mary Gilkerson, Annie Hitselberger Fell, Tammy Wilkins Jenkins,
Elizabeth Akin Stelling, Virginia Clare Andrews, Amy Coquillard, Coralee
Harris, Kate Fox, Janet Hull

My Prayer to Saint Francis

Francis, I confess, reality can be a Big Gulp cup.
My dreams of Christmas often end up in the rain.

Enlightenment can come from a silver-spooned buffoon.
Truth can deflate from transcendent to simple acceptance.

Oh, mesmerizing bald man with a bird in the square window,
Teach me to blow my pink throat with the calm of the anole.

Let me taste the bitter anise and enjoy it and call it sweet.
Crazy man who slept with a wolf, teach me to be a master of peace.

May my desire to shine not eclipse my humble wish.
May I crave bliss less than the ability to celebrate this:

Cool weather that will suddenly develop into humidity,
The expectation of warm reverence that turns so chilly,

Loving eyes that go from mesmerize to gut-punching blind,
Faith that unravels its skein from a pattern of castoff to gnostic,

And constant care of others that scratches character, exhausted.
I want to love these. I want to be like the seed you defenestrate

Turbulent, that feeds your feathered friends who fly with little weight.
Cup and throat, rain and pain, seed and bird, state and change:

Let me be all of these in life, show me how to be variable
and still at ease, and still at peace, and still be, and grateful.

Co-Created with Charlotte Koon Ehney, Joyce Norman, Mildred Speidel, Keith Bates, James St John, Laura Gaffke, Robert CJ Graves, Sandy Mau, Anne Nichols Miller, Louise M Greer, Diane Hare, Kirill Simin, Annmarie Lockhart, Tommy Lightfoot, Helen Summer, Norma Jeane Tiner, Feili Tu-Keefner, Janeen Musselman, Lisa Gornicki Bolender, Kris Friend, Cindy Patterson, Tammy Wilkins Jenkins, Christine Tapson, Barbara H Thomson, Veronica Dangerfield, Camille Richardson, Al Black, Lisa Nielsen, Lisa Rynex Ragusa, Marguerite O'Brien, Pamela Cauthen Meriwether, Jeanette Cheezum

What the Moon Said as She Was Leaving

Everything spectacular is broken.
Like a pearl that ruins the shell it opens
Birthing its alabaster dharma to awaken.

You are broken like this.
You are ready to awaken, too.

Everything scared starts as penumbra.
Shadow serves a banquet at the table
Where lunatic fringe sits next to karma.

You are scared like this.
You are also eating this meal through.

Everything pensive gets convoluted.
Hallelujah sings jazz about the difference
As we prepare to leave and rise to apogee and soar.

You are stuck like this.
You are ready to end the war.

Everything refulgent is molten at its core.
Sequestration doesn't ever really work
Because hearts can open doors.

You are a house on fire like this.
You are the ceiling and the floor.

Every crash comes from lack of focus.
A newspaper reports the voluptuous,
And the chaos, cacophony, and score.

You are distracted like this.
You are ready for so much more.

Every jam potentially produces juice.
Turn that tourniquet loose to find that
Earth has grapes and moon has olivine.

You are fruit and round and sweet like this.
You grow and you change and you are wine.

Co-Created with Tamela Spires Hastie, Cindy Patterson, Coralee Harris, Elyn Blackman, Marguerite O'Brien, Corrie Struble, Jeanne Porter Ashley, Susanne Kappler, Trish Vicino, Mary Ann Joseph, Jules Ellinger Hunt, Amy Alley, Carla Blankenship Mangine, Louise M Greer, Barbara H Thomson, Libby Bussinah, Annmarie Lockhart, Ann Poling, Janet Hull, Lisa Nielsen, Jeanette Cheezum, Helen Summer, Elizabeth JoAnn Sumner Jones, Feili Tu-Keefner, Julianna Temple-Roberts, Joyce Norman, Worthy Branson Evans, Bruce Clark, Al Black, Kathy Paget

Holy Christmas! Eight crazy nights! What a year this has been!

Anyone else feel like latkes fried and a bit burnt and warming in the oven?
Like this has been a twelve-month lesson in hope amidst conundrum?

Here, Dear, is a list of what we want this year: Optimism at the exact moment
when the foundation on which our lives are planted shifts and opens.

Clarity when our expectation is hit by a hurricane and all the doors
are locked and we are in a loony bin. Wonderment the minute

the buried dirt bubbles from below to release the clandestine
from those we think we know. And all we can do is burst

into laughter and cry HO HO HO! Belief. Even so. Warmth
from within when we are out of wood. Reconciliation

with all that's good. Joy that goes beyond nostalgia into
a releasing of the doubt and guilt and should. One tingle.

One jingle. All of us, every one, learning how to intermingle.
Our renewal of faith in life and earth and love and personhood.

Co-Created with Jessica Leigh Wells, Amy Alley, Daniel Dowe, Coralee Harris,
Terri Lynn Mac McLaughlin, Kris Friend, Kimberley Goeglein Puryear, Annmarie
Lockhart, Rebecca C Jacobson, Laurel Posey, Kezia Slaughter, Diane Hare,
Ellen Parker Dukes, Leisa Marie Mounts, Gail McGrail Glasser, Lisa Nielsen,
Casey Catherine Moore, Louise M Greer, Kathy Paget, Duna Miller, Val Ryan,
Julianna Temple-Roberts

Penultimate

This is my second-to-last poem of the year
(because I simplify and stay off-line over
Christmas), and I don't want to be pompous
but I've got some things I've been waiting
for ages to get off my chest. (You, reader,
will remain anonymous, I promise.)

                To you, who do
the tootsie-roll (the dance, you know who
you are) while you leave chance behind
and choose to intoxicate: Wait. Hold up.
Stop the lackadaisical way you avoid
fate. It's simple. Pull your own weight.
We all carry freight.

                And to those who
are blessed and somehow feel this rises
you above the rest, like God has his hand
in your puppet and this gives you uplift,
try this: pick up a jinriksha and take a
mountain trip. See how quick the exotic
turns prosaic and the light grows heavy
in such juxtaposing wit. Meditate on that
shit.

    Now for the scandalous among us,
those who eat too many cookies or are
addicted to bleaching the bum or get
exuberant at the thought of eating sushi
or whatever release you wreak when

it all is done: Relax. You are fine. No
need to retaliate against your craving.
You are no monster. In time, you will
learn to slow down, hang out. Be a
windchime. In the meantime, have fun.

                              Enfin,
I address those who want life to be a
journey to an enchanted destination,
who live in awe of the strength of
their own ideas, who want logic and
call and response and effect after cause:
I'm sorry to break it like this, but
this existence is more baffling than
that. And simple, too. God is a
toddler who got loose with the
glitter and glue. And made you.
And the tootsie-roll dancers, and
the bored and the blessed, the
jinriksha drivers, and the overeaters
and the hot mess. We are all the
penultimate draft. So sit back.
Let go in love. No judge. Hug.
And thank you for letting me get
this off my merry cookie-filled chest.

Co-Created with Janet Hull, Lisa Rynex Ragusa, Gail McGrail Glasser, Helen
Summer, Carol Brady, Barbie Smith Mathis, Barbara H Thomson, Lisa Nielsen,
Tommy Lightfoot, Bruce Clark, Liz Cunningham Delp, Kris Friend, Mildred Speidel,
Mary Hutchins Harris, Candi Padget, Melinda Oliver, Elizabeth JoAnn Sumner
Jones, Tammy Wilkins Jenkins, Debbie Turner, Amaryllis Turman, Joyce Norman,
Lisa Gornicki Bolender, Rachel Onley, Kathy Paget, Charles Steven, Feili Tu-Keefner,
Carol Agnew Black, Leisa Marie Mounts, James St John, Linda Tina Maldonado,
Southcarolina Artists, Louise M Greer, Kathie Turner, Ellen Kline McLeod, Al Black,
Mike Amason, Cara Holman, Jeanette Cheezum, Jeanne Porter Ashley

The Season of Acceptance Is Upon Us

The season of acceptance is upon us;
we throw ourselves into letting go
of all we could not change this year.

Sitting still beneath that tree and facing
the root of our fear while opening
to the possibility that the greatest
gift of all is to be who we are and
to love from that same deep place.

Change like this happens at a glacial
pace, but this body's life is not a race.

Honey is sweeter than water, for instance,
because it is thicker and more viscous.

Both can be heated until fervent, as can
our hearts. Any element or part made fiery
too quickly can burn, though, as our ancient
ones did know about trysts becoming tristful
(Latin: tristis; French: triste: Late Middle
English [think Chaucer]: trystefull.)

Out of such a tryst were we born bodily,
as was he. Seeing the miracle of this
is called awakening, which is not only
possible, but happens every morning.

The season of acceptance is upon us;
we throw ourselves into letting go
of all we could not change this year.

Sitting still beneath that tree and facing
the root of everything while believing
in the possibility that the greatest
gift of all has already been given.
We are who we are wholly, and we are
wholly loved from our depths to our stars.

CoCreated with Lizzie Thomas, Virginia Clare Andrews, Pamela Barnett, Karen Fuchs, Annmarie Lockhart, Christi Stewart, Kimberley Goeglein Puryear, Corey Mesler, Janet Hull, Betty Cobb Gurnell, Kezia Slaughter

Ever After

Rebirth

It takes great strength to breathe.
It comes from within. An open
grin. You have to be willing
to give. This is restorative.
This is renewal. This often
happens twice. Once, healing
the adversity of life. Again,
for the cartwheel of wife.

We begin as snow. Melting
helps us to grow. Soon we flow
into waterfall and quench all
the tulips below. It takes faith.
You must learn to translate.
Pri(smi)ck, for example, has
prism and smile in it. And
the ( ) separating is from ick.

Awakening is like this. A new
language that comes not from
one country, but from both.
And the ocean between them
dives deep into blue growth.
You are no gypsy. You belong
to me. Like the sunrise I see
in your eyes. It shines for me.

Other words, like déjà vu and
touché, mean "we." Enlighten
is to see. And then we make a
promise. No mayhem, only
yes-ness. All tomorrow under

a fig tree. All wants becoming
once. No rampage. No pithy.
Yes/no perception with clarity.

Joy. Renewed like pollen that
gets under our skin. Feeds the
blossoming within. Comes out
as a rainbow. Is perfect and
perfectly content to let it show.
This is mercy. Life. Love. This
is what we came from above
to come here to do. This is
grace. Our zephyrean embrace.

Co-Created with Mary Yanni, Alan Altshuld, Christi Stewart, Dayna Smith, Laura Gaffke, Clarissa McFairy, Alison Beard, Cheryl Anne Cudmore, Gail McGrail Glasser, Laura MacLean, Candi Padgett, Linda Clotfelter, Nicola Waldron, Amy Coquillard, Al Black, Elizabeth JoAnn Sumner Jones, Kyra Strasberg, Tamela Spires Hastie, Libby Bussinah, Rene Smith, Ruth Parks Andrew, Daniel Dowe, Kris Friend, Betty Cobb Gurnell, Charlotte Koon Ehney, Caroline Flow, Wendy Zhang, Chie Guenther, Jeanette Gallagher, Blanche Premo-Hopkins, Daves Here Man, Kate Hammerich, Susanne Kappler

My God

"You know what he [Meister Eckhart] said? The only thing
that burns in Hell is the part of you that won't let go of
your life; your memories, your attachments. They burn
'em all away. But they're not punishing you, he said.
They're freeing your soul.... If you're frightened of dying
and holding on, you'll see devils tearing your life away.
But if you've made your peace then the devils are really
angels, freeing you."

—Jacob's
Ladder

My God starts out as mercy. The Daddy.
Then he leaves. And you are kind of
happy.

My God then wanders
in a red coat in winter sacrificing her
little body.

My God appears in a hailstorm
that freezes the private parts and makes
you run for home.

My God
is hesitant. Gets good grades
in grad school. Be good. Be good.

My God is magnificent. She
bows down and plants a baby
in me.

My God is an accomplishment.
Push, push, go, more, more.
Go.

My God is is is is is is is is
repeat.

My God is an avocado
on thighs and fingers
and teeth and tongues.

My God is a sequel
I read
over
and
over.

My God is Meister.
Franciscans came after him
for saying God is fecund.

My God crossed
the Avignon bridge with me
and I sang with my husband
and daughter and we danced
and shook that Pont d'Avignon
until I felt the Vatican river
below me and it splashed
up and blessed us
three.

Wednesday

My God is a lion.
She taught me to rest
  in the grass and to hunt
  for what lasts
  fiercely.

  My God. My God.
My God blesses me.

Co-Created with Annmarie Lockhart, Kristi Krumnow Fulhriman, Alice Shapiro, Joyce Norman, Lisa Nielsen, Louise M Greer, Jeannette Cheezum, Marguerite O'Brien, Debbie Turner

 **Cassie Premo Steele, PhD,** is a poet, writer, and Co-Creating coach with two decades of experience teaching in university and community settings. Her poetry has been nominated three times for a Pushcart Prize. She gave a 2013 TEDx Talk on "Writing as a Way of Calming, Centering, and Making Meaning." *Wednesday*, the world's first social media co-created poetry book, is her eleventh book publication. Her website is www.cassiepremosteele.com.

What people are saying about *Wednesday*:

What an innovative use of social media and collaboration to bring the art of writing poetry alive!

—Virginia J. Pulver

Cassie Premo Steele's *Wednesday* is fun, clever, and interesting! I am always amazed at what she is able to come up with using so many word contributions!

—Kezia Willingham

Wednesday is a creative compilation of the minds and words of many beautiful people harnessed by the intuition, imagination, and literary skill of the one and only Cassie Premo Steele. It has been a light amidst every week—an inspiration and a joy.

—Melinda Oliver

Wednesday has been a great spark to start my day—it gets my creative juices going by playing with the words that jump to mind immediately and sorting through them until I find just the "right" one. I even titled a painting of mine, using my word for that day—it was perfect—and probably wouldn't have occurred to me otherwise.

—Libby Bussinah

Wednesday infuses freedom of expression with poetic genius!

—Elizabeth JoAnn Sumner Jones

Wednesday to me is a combination of friends, feelings and words brought together through the raw, impeccable talent of Cassie Premo Steele.

—Kathie Turner

Wednesday is pure fun! It inspires my heart when reading others' creative thoughts.

—Lisa Hills

How can one person put the collective awesomeness of *Wednesday* in one quote? To keep with the one word theme: FANTASTIC!

—*Leisa Marie Mounts*

Wednesday inspires creativity through collaboration, unites a varied group of strangers with the power of one word and Cassie Premo Steele's eloquent writing. *Wednesday* brings joy and fun to a disparate band of writers.

—*Kris Friend*

Wednesday—a glimpse at co-creation fun!

—*Gail McGrail Glasser*

Wednesday is a collection of multiple individuals' one-word thoughts brought together creatively by our poet, the amazing Cassie. Most of us have never met, yet still we are able to come together as one, join our words—the result? Always a knock-out piece of poetry that none of us, alone, could render.

—*Joyce Norman*

Cassie Premo Steele crafts our individual words—our diverse thoughts and images—into a coherent treasure! That is the magic of a poet!

—*Charlotte Koon Ehney*

Wednesday by Cassie Premo Steele is a compendium of weekly co-created poems, village word art that pulls the blanket off of what we are all thinking.

—*Janet Hull*

Humpalicious!

—*Nicola Waldron*

Other Titles by unbound CONTENT

A Strange Frenzy
By Dom Gabrielli

At Age Twenty
By Maxwell Baumbach

Before the Great Troubling
By Corey Mesler

Elegy
By Raphaela Willington

Assumption
By Jim Davis

Painting Czeslawa Kwoka
By Theresa Senato Edwards and Lori Schreiner

Saltian
By Alice Shapiro

The Pomegranate Papers
By Cassie Premo Steele

and many more.

Browse our bookshelf:
unboundcontent.com